Table of Contents

LeRoy Collins
Leon County Public Library
200 W. Park Avenue
Tallahassee, Fl 32301

Foreword

Just think what your home would be like without soft, touchable textiles. No other decorating tool offers such a range of color and mood-setting pattern—from solids in vibrant bursts of pigment or gentle, hushed tones, to prints that seem to whisper a soft lullaby, hum a cheerful melody or sing out in a rousing crescendo. Yes, fabric is the soft side of decorating, the component that turns a house into a comfortable, welcoming, gorgeous home!

Whether you're looking forward to new window treatments, bed coverings or accent pieces, there's a seemingly endless array of fabric options open to you today. A trip to a fabric store reveals bolt after bolt of prints and solids, naturals and synthetics, neutrals and brights. It's a challenge to choose one, let alone select a well-coordinated grouping!

If you feel a bit overwhelmed at the prospect of decorating your home with fabric, this book may be your lifesaver. *Fabric All Through The House* offers tips for choosing colors, materials and prints—professional advice to help you put together a palette and mix and match patterns in your home.

Chock-full of color photos, this book will show you many examples of beautifully decorated rooms. Then, you'll witness the transformation of a newly purchased condominium, a blank slate that now boasts a coordinated selection of striking fabric decor. (This project was put together by an amateur decorator on a budget—someone, perhaps, a little bit like you.)

Each of the condominium's fabric features will be accompanied by easy-to-follow instructions. You can copy or customize any of the projects to suit your own personal style.

Happy decorating!

Nature has certainly supplied us all with an abundance of beautiful, glowing color, and aren't we enriched? Without warm, vivid orange, brilliant yellow and vibrant red, what pleasure would we find in a sunset?

About Color

Hue is the lightness or darkness of a color.

Intensity is the brightness or dullness of a color.

Temperature is the warm or cool quality of a color.

Yes, there's no doubt about it, we inhabit a colorful world. In this and following pages, you'll learn more about color and how to make it work in your home.

Interior designers are well versed in the language of color—they know their way around a color wheel—and if you're decorating or redecorating, it will help if you know a bit about this subject too.

The basic color wheel is made up of 12 colors:

The primaries red, blue and yellow, are the hues from which the others originate.

Secondary colors orange, green and purple are created by mixing the primaries.

Intermediate colors are the result of mixing primary and secondary colors: yellow-orange, red-orange, red-violet, blue-green and yellow-green.

These 12 colors and the true neutrals, white, black and gray, are the basis of every other color mix. (If you're wondering about the brown family, these shades are actually versions of oranges, yellows and reds.)

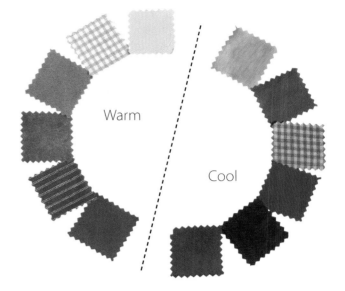

To determine which of the basic wheel colors are warm or cool, divide the circle in half. The colors on the left side of yellow-green are warm and those to the right of red-violet are cool.

Both green and violet are considered "bridging colors" because they are made up of both warm and cool shades. Green comes from the mix of warm yellow and cool blue and violet is created by warm red and cool blue. Thus, these two color families can help balance the temperature in either a warm or cool color scheme.

If you're a fan of neutrals, you have more to choose from than ever before with new neutrals. These are traditional colors that have been muted to an extremely low intensity until the color is effectively neutralized. For example, consider a purple so deep it's almost black, or a dark gray with the tiniest hint of green.

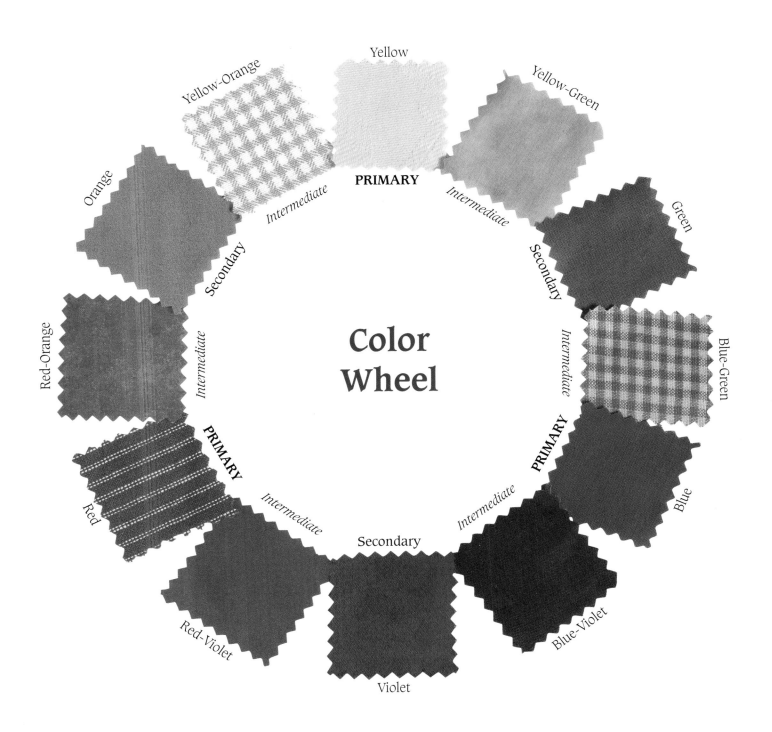

Color Wheel

Yellow — **PRIMARY**

Yellow-Orange — *Intermediate*

Orange — **Secondary**

Red-Orange — *Intermediate*

Red — **PRIMARY**

Red-Violet — *Intermediate*

Violet — Secondary

Blue-Violet — *Intermediate*

Blue — **PRIMARY**

Blue-Green — *Intermediate*

Green — **Secondary**

Yellow-Green — *Intermediate*

If the colors in a traditional color wheel don't seem typical of the ones you would select for your pillows or curtains, it may be because of their intensity. These are pure, clear, bright colors, whereas you might prefer the muted shades, pastels, or darker versions. It helps to think of your preferred shades of these colors when looking at the wheel. Your green might be "forest" or "sage", your yellow-orange a pale peach and your red, a soft pink.

Now, you're an expert on color. Are you ready to learn how to make it work for you?

Using Colors

Unless you're a professional decorator, you're probably among the many who are a little nervous about choosing a palette for your home. Nobody wants to put a lot of time, effort and money into window treatments, bed covers or accent pillows only to find they don't "go" with the sofa or rug. One thing to keep in mind as you choose colors is you don't have to follow color trends. Use the colors you love, the ones that make you feel happy or peaceful. Remember, no two people see color exactly the same way.

Here are a few more important pieces of advice to consider when you're working with color and pattern.

1. You don't have to match colors perfectly. First of all, it's extremely difficult to find a perfect match, even if you have paint professionally mixed to go with your couch fabric. Color on the wall looks different than color in fabric because of the differences in texture. Similarly, color "reads" brighter or lighter on a shiny fabric than a heavily textured one. Also, colors can have an effect on each other. Yellow interspersed in a blue and white pattern will look slightly different than a solid yellow that covers an expansive wall.

2. Almost any colors can be combined as long as you keep them in the same intensity or value.

Picture a room done in rainbow pastels, utilizing light blue, yellow, mint green, peach and lavender. It works because they're all light, or the same value.

Or how about a room done in amethyst, ruby, gold and emerald—a mix of jewel tones of the same deep, dark value?

Once you've followed this rule, it's time to break it, just a little. Add the surprise of a brighter orange or purple to the pastel room in the form of small accents—a pillow and a couple of vases. This will add interest and make you look like a professional decorator!

3. Use unequal quantities of different colors. Whether you're using different shades of the same color family or a mix of three or four different hues or patterns, it's important to choose one as dominant, then compliment and accent with the others. In general, an equal amount of different colors will fight for attention (though this may be the look you want for a playful child's room).

Complimentary Colors

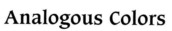

Our color wheel can be helpful in choosing colors that compliment, enhance and blend. Colors opposite or approximately opposite on the ring are complimentary. They intensify each other, or as some designers say, create visual "energy." Some classic compliments include green and red (think mint and rose) blue and red, and yes, blue and orange, which includes that southwest standard, turquoise and terra cotta.

Analogous Colors

Analogous colors are related colors that lie side by side on the color wheel and make an eye-pleasing scheme when combined. Blues and greens share similar cool, restful qualities and work well together, just as yellows and oranges (such as coral or clay) offer a beaming tribute to a warm, cheery scene. Just remember, it's best to vary the quantities, focusing on either yellow or orange, and using the other as an accent, perhaps with a little warm, sage green thrown in as well.

Complex

Complex Color Scheme

If you use three or four colors spaced in an equidistant pattern around the color ring, you're using a complex color scheme. This can be a little more difficult, but the rule of similar values or intensities makes it easier. A floral pattern of dusty rose, muted lilac and lichen green can be enhanced by a swag in a dusty rose/honey-yellow check. A rose-tinted neutral on the wall keeps the emphasis on one color, as would a solid fabric on a footstool.

Other Color Schemes

Other color schemes include monochromatic, with which you indulge your love of a favorite color to your heart's content. If it's green, you take nature's cue and use a variety of green shades. This color particularly lends itself to a monochromatic scheme, since greens tend to blend together indoors as well as they do outside. With a monochromatic scheme, pattern is the key to creating interest. Mix several tone-on-tone fabrics, varying the color values from light to medium to dark.

Pattern interplay is also the trick when you decorate with neutral and new neutral colors. Mix numerous patterns, textures and finishes to add richness to a living room bedecked in quiet taupes and grays.

Neutral shades are perfect additions to virtually any color scheme. Decorator wisdom says every room needs a bit of black, which serves to clarify the other colors and anchor the room.

White (or off white) is essential to almost any color mix. White is clean, fresh and unobtrusive, and it adds crispness to other colors. Think of the cheer of yellow and white, the breezy, well-loved look of blue and white and the classically crisp red, white and blue. White offers a welcoming place for the eye to rest and is a great background unifier when you want to combine several patterns.

Black and white is a classic combination, lively, yet sophisticated and easy to enhance with any number of bright or deep hues.

Photo courtesy of Calico Corners

A crisp blue and white color scheme.

An all white color scheme is sophisticated and contemporary, and according to "feng shui" philosophy, the pathway to true harmony. White is the perfect backdrop for a colorful art collection or a grouping of bright antiques. If you want to show off the unique lines of modern art-inspired furniture, dark walls and white upholstery can create a virtual sculpture gallery.

If you're planning to decorate or redecorate several rooms or the whole house, professionals advise that you pick up some of your palette colors in adjoining rooms. You might use different intensities of the same colors or emphasize a different one in the dining room than you did in the living room, but if you want your decor scheme to flow, it's best to use color to tie the rooms together in an open floor plan.

Conversely, if lots of diverse color is your goal in a contemporary decorating scheme, perhaps you want to reverse this rule and offer the surprise of a different, bold color in every room of the house!

Photo courtesy of Calico Corners

If you want your decor scheme to flow, pick up some of your palette colors from adjoining rooms.

7

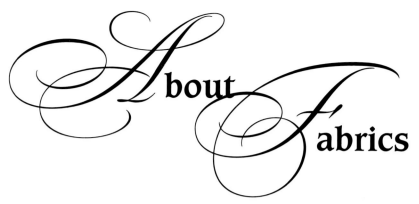

About Fabrics

Selecting Fabrics

It can be difficult enough to determine the color scheme you want for your new kitchen or bathroom, but then you have the task of choosing fabrics as well! There are so many beautiful prints and solids, and they come in a wide variety of materials. Cotton, linen, chintz or rayon, how do you select the perfect fabric for your curtains, pillows and stool covers?

If durability is an important concern, bear in mind that fabrics with a tight weave and high thread count per square inch will hold up best. Look for an even texture without ribs or raised fibers and consider the manufacturer's instructions for fiber content and care.

The chart below offers information about a number of popular fabrics, providing tips for care and the types of home decorating projects for which they're suited:

Natural Fiber Fabrics

FABRIC TYPE	QUALITIES	USES	CARE
Cotton	Absorbent, dyes well, drapes well, little elasticity, blends well with other fibers. Comes in a variety of weights. Heavy cotton such as twill, canvas, denim and ticking is quite durable, while lighter weights can be sheer.	Great for just about any sewing project. Ideal for window treatments. Heavy cotton is just right for washable slipcovers.	Very easy to clean. Wash or dry clean. Iron at high temperatures. Wash fabric before cutting to allow for shrinkage.
Muslin	A soft, woven cotton. Can be light or heavyweight, bleached or unbleached. Inexpensive. Tends to shrink.	Muslin makes a nice drape for casual decor schemes.	Wash fabric before cutting. Best to hand wash in cold water.
Chintz	A tightly woven cotton fabric with a glazed or polished finish. Can be quilted and embossed. Chintz is crisp, but gets softer with each washing.	Lovely for valances, shades and other window treatments that don't require a lot of drape. Also for pillows, cushions, slipcovers, bedspreads.	Dry clean to preserve finish. Apply a drop of iodine to a small swatch. If it turns brown, the finish is permanent. If blue, it isn't.
Linen	Woven from flax plant material. Comes in various weights, dyes well, doesn't stretch, resists sun damage and moths. Blends well with other fabrics, which adds strength and durability.	Offers a natural look for drapes, and once pressed, holds a tight crease for pleats. Linen pillows can be embellished with natural materials for a decorative look. Makes a nice duvet cover when blended with cotton.	Dry clean. Iron, using high temperatures.
Silk	Made with fiber from silkworms. Drapes well, doesn't sag and resists wrinkling and mildew Holds brightly colored dyes. Not as durable as some fabrics..	Perfect for swags and drapes, but a lining is recommended for durability. Makes lovely pillows with added beading and trim.	Dry clean only. Iron, using medium temperature.

Synthetic Fiber Fabrics

FABRIC TYPE	QUALITIES	USES	CARE
Polyester	Made of a filament fiber from petroleum by-products. Resists wrinkling and moths. Quite durable, and makes a wonderful fabric when blended with cotton.	Work well for draperies and valances. Holds ruffles, gathers, soft folds.	Wash or dry clean. Iron on low temperature.
Voile	A highly twisted combination of natural and synthetic fibers, often cotton and polyester. Voile is lightweight and crisp, but delicate.	Makes sheer window treatments that provide better than average light control and privacy. Can be used for swags and jabots when self-lined.	Cold wash in a short cycle. Iron on low setting.
Damask	Reversible damask is a combination of plain and satin weaves, often utilizing silk, linen, cotton, and/or rayon.	Heavy damasks are used for formal draperies and upholstery. Not a good choice for a casual, breezy ambience.	Read care label on fabric bolt. Otherwise, dry clean.
Taffeta	Tightly woven, crisp fabric combined with other fibers for increased pliability. Creases easily and is best used by a more experienced seamstress. Water or steam leaves a permanent stain, so shouldn't be washed or steam cleaned.	Formal draperies and valances, perfect to embellish with trims and tassels. Best used in a room where children and pets aren't the rule. If blended with acetate, not for use in the bathroom.	Press from the wrong side, using a press cloth to avoid seam impressions.
Velvet	Nap or pile fabric with a woven background. Made mainly with silk or rayon pile and cotton back. Soft and durable with a noticeable sheen.	No longer just for formal settings, velvet is popping up everywhere. Use it for bedding, drapes, pillows, slipcovers and upholstery.	Dry clean. Steam, but never press. Dirt can be brushed away with a vacuum.
Brocade	A mid to heavy weight, jacquard-weave fabric with a pattern (usually floral) that appears to be raised. This is because the design is woven in contrasting colors or weaves, such as silk, cotton, wool, etc. is a bit heavier than brocade.	Draperies and valances in a formal living room or master suite. Looks luxurious and expensive, and it usually is!	Dry clean and spot clean, as needed.
Rayon	Inexpensive fabric made from recycled cellulose. Resists moths and static electricity. Doesn't hold a shape, but still great for windows because it drapes well and is very soft. Holds bright dyes.	Not suitable for pleated drapes, but works well for simple valances, swags and panels.	Check label on fabric bolt. Usually wash before cutting, then hand wash in mild detergent and rinse thoroughly. Press on wrong side, medium temperature.
Lace	A web of threads creates this openwork fabric. Can be very fragile, but mistakes can be hidden. There are hundreds of different types of lace.	Lace fabric makes curtains, such as double pocket sheers, tablecloths, even wall hangings suitable for a glass frame. Lining lace helps stabilize it for window treatments. Lace also is used to embellish pillows, bed linens, etc.	A few can be machine washed and dried, but most need to be dry cleaned.
Tapestry	Heavy, woven fabric with a pictorial or other design. Stiff and heavy with a rough surface. Can be expensive.	Often used for wall hangings, but also works well for drapes. Makes a nice cover for a piano or other stool, and is sometimes used for upholstery.	Dry clean only.
Acetate	Made from regenerated cellulose fibers. Drapes beautifully and is resistant to sunlight damage. Dries quickly.	Makes a wide variety of window treatments. Gives a formal look, but the drapes are durable.	Can be machine washed or dry cleaned.
Sheers	Lightweight, transparent fabric, which can include voile, lace, gossamer, organdy, chiffon and muslin. Can include embroidery, beading and appliques. Softly diffuses light.	Excellent for swags and window panels. Works well in conjunction with shades or blinds, or as a decorative accent to a window. Sheers make wonderful bed canopies.	Follow manufacturer's instructions. Depending on fiber content, can often be washed.

Textiles are colorful, multi-textured, and wonderful to the touch, but what really sets fabric apart from other decorating tools is pattern. Scenic toiles, lush florals, cheerful gingham checks and eye-catching stripes combine with brilliant or whisper-soft solids to create an endless array of decorative fabric options.

Combining fabrics

Just as it can be a bit daunting to choose a color palette, the prospect of pattern combining puts some people into a panic. But, just as it is with color, there are a variety of ways to mix and match prints.

Pattern can be put into three basic categories by the size, or scale, of the design motifs. In a **medium pattern**, you can see the individual design components even when viewing the fabric from across the room. A **small-scale** design looks solid or textured from a distance, while the details of a **large print** can be readily viewed even from an adjacent room.

medium pattern

small scale

large print

Generally, it is best to avoid using two patterns of the same scale, and it's better to combine small and medium or medium and large rather than pairing a tiny print with a large design. When working with a bold pattern, stick to a larger scale project to show it off. Its design might be wasted on a pillow, but really make a statement on a large tablecloth.

Keep in mind that the larger the piece, the bolder the pattern or color will appear. An intensely colored or patterned fabric swatch may be exciting, but will you feel overwhelmed by it when it covers your sofa and love seat?

If you want to combine three or more fabric patterns in a room, a good rule of thumb is to stick to solid or subtly textured colors on walls and floors.

Pattern Play

Unify fabric patterns by color

The way to unify different fabric patterns is through–you guessed it–color! Exact matches aren't necessary, but colors that are similar and of the same intensity or value make for harmonious pattern blends. At least one color in a dominant fabric pattern should be picked up by supporting patterns.

If you have two patterns of equal scale that you'd really love to combine, it helps if both have a white background as well as echoing colors. White is a great unifier, and gives the eye designated areas of rest between the stimulating print designs.

If you want to combine three or more fabric patterns in a room, a good rule of thumb is to stick to solid or subtly textured colors on walls and floors. This creates a sense of balance and helps avoid a dizzying feeling. Keeping accessories to a minimum works well here, also. A neutral color scheme offers a perfect backdrop for multiple pattern and texture combinations—all in variations of the same gray, taupe, white or new neutrals, or a mix of a few. This also holds true for monochromatic decorating, where you might freely combine checks, stripes, dots and whimsical patterns without a care. If you follow these basic rules, even the smallest room can carry off an energetic mix of patterns.

Now, isn't it time you got going?

1. Gather ideas

If you don't have a decorating scheme in mind, then you're open to suggestions. Be on the lookout for ideas when you visit friends' homes, furniture stores or model homes and jot them down in a notebook. Keep a clip file for pictures you find in magazines and catalogues.

2. Match existing pieces

Make note of any permanent pieces already existing in your room or rooms. If you're planning to keep the rug, paint, or a favorite leather armchair, the color and texture may be the starting point from which you launch your palette. At the very least, the "keepers" need to blend in with your newly decorated pieces.

3. Assess your color scheme

If you're going to make just a few changes, but want them to have maximum impact, first make an assessment of the colors you're using in your home now. Go from room to room and write down the colors you see starting with the most dominant and ending with the smallest accents.

Once this is done, see if you can determine your home's palette, using the color information in previous chapters. Now, is there a color that might tie a room together, or perhaps one you'd like to pick up from an adjoining room to add to the flow of your floor plan?

4. Choose your palette

If you're starting from scratch, ask yourself some questions. Determine which are the colors you love, which make you most comfortable or happy. Perhaps it's a color you most often wear or one that reminds you of a favorite place or pastime. Or, choose a color scheme that will convey a mood to suit a specific room. A sunny or dramatic kitchen is a great place to start the day, while a soothing, calm bedroom promotes rest and relaxation.

5. Work around a favorite fabric or accessory

If you love your couch and want to decorate around it, you have a ready-made palette to work with. A painting, rug, wallpaper or even a favorite item of clothing can be used as a substitute for a key fabric, anything that you can bring with you and use to coordinate.

Some people are inspired by their collectibles, building a room around a collection of blue willow porcelain or chintzware, for instance.

6. Visit a paint store

Bring your key fabric or other inspiration to a paint store. Select paint-sample cards, each offering several variations of a paint shade.

Choose samples to approximately match every color in your key. If you don't have something to work around, choose paint cards in the colors you're thinking about using.

If you want to use a variety of colors, you'll want the shades to be in the same position on each sample card (e.g. second from top)—that way they'll be the same value and intensity. If you desire a monochromatic scheme, choose colors that are separated by one shade, as this will provide more interest than hues that are too close.

7. Visit fabric stores

Choose fabrics to approximately match your paint samples, freely selecting a wide variety of patterns and solids. Some prints might have all or most of your chosen colors, while others will just emphasize one or two. Fabric stores display their decorator fabrics in color groups—with solids, prints, plaids and checks all on one rack. You might discover your entire selection of fabrics all in one place! Ask the clerk to cut small samples for you, or if you'd like bigger swatches, consider buying 1/4 yard of each to take home. If you find a fabric you know you want, take it outside to view it in a different light before purchasing.

8. Study your samples at home

Lay all your samples in a cluster, including paint chips, if applicable, then stand back and look at them. Take some fabrics away and try different combinations. Weed out any immediate rejects. If two are very similar, choose the one you prefer and place the other, at least temporarily, in the discard pile. From the remaining selection, determine your palette. If it's very cool or warm, maybe you'd like to add a bridging color for balance. If it's complimentary, you need to alter the quantities of different colors for a more pleasing look. It could be too sedate or too bold, and need an additional accent color to harmonize.

9. View your samples from a distance

When you have a grouping you think you like, place them in the target room. Some will look better when they're not side by side, so separate them with a solid or neutral. You'll want to distribute patterns throughout the room rather than cluster several in one corner. Viewed from 10 - 12 feet away, your eye tends to mix the colors in a pattern, so lavender and white might look purple-pink. Are you pleased with the palette you see? If you'll be making pillows for an existing sofa, place the fabric on the furniture, perhaps wrapped around an existing pillow, then observe.

10. Make a sample board

Make a sample board for each room you'll be decorating. Lay fabric swatch cut-outs and paint chips together on poster board and leave them sitting out for awhile. Watch what happens as the light changes throughout the day and how the colors look at night, under artificial light. If you still love your selections, you've made a decision!

The professionally decorated rooms photographed and compiled for the following chapter will provide you with a bit of inspiration for your own projects. Of course, textiles are the star in each setting, including sumptuous draperies, upholstery, pillows, wall covering, bed linens and more. Whenever possible, a closer look at some of the fabrics used, as well as specific information about them, is provided.

As you look at each picture, note the color scheme, decorating style and pattern interplay in the room. Would the look fit your lifestyle? What do you like or dislike about each room? Then, feel free to borrow some of the ideas or color schemes and make them your own. Refer to the index for general instructions, for some of these basic treatments.

Living Rooms

This formal living room is a sunny, floral fantasy, abloom in a mix of rich color. The draperies, chair and ottoman flaunt a lush, garden-print damask in a warm palette that combines shades of coral and yellow-green on a golden ground. The solid damask sofa provides an anchor, an interlude of subtly-textured color accenting the hues in the floral pattern.

The second chair is upholstered in a delightful cotton toile in a dusky coral shade with gold accents. Many toiles and florals blend beautifully, and this one plays a harmonious supporting role to the dominant fabric. The toile is also picked up on a cameo pillow on the sofa, where a charming medallion is circled with a tassel trim.

Other accent pillows include two in a color-coordinating, smaller floral print accessorized with braid and tassel trims. The textured chair pillow picks up the green and peach in the two floral patterns.

Adding to the stately grandeur of the room, the curtains are highlighted with a Murphy valance knotted with decorative cording. The contrasting lining can be seen beneath the softly cascading folds at the sides.

The window treatments play a starring role in this grand room, which boasts an expanse of glass panes that stretch almost from floor to ceiling. An undulating cascade of color serves as a dramatic backdrop for the near-neutral furniture and rug palette.

Goblet-pleated draperies offer cool, green tones along with complimentary shades of red, lilac and other accents. The inside edges are embellished with a brush fringe and each pleat is topped with silk-covered buttons. These drapes share the spotlight with balloon shades in coordinating plaid, the crisp silk fabric holding perfect poufs.

What pulls this look together? The exquisite sofa pillows—each an individual work of art. Together, they make a decorative statement, providing a perfect transition between the white sofa and color-drenched windows.

The pillows are made with a variety of silk and cotton blends framed with beading, tassels, cording and ruffles. Each adds to the green and neutral scheme, with rose and other accents picked up as well.

*A*colorful, antique toy theme suggested the palette for this welcoming room. Fresh blues and yellows are dominant here, with generous supporting accents from the green and red families. Though the palette is primary, note that the similar value and intensity of the colors make the room energetic, yet soothing at the same time.

Framed by yellow and white "damask" print wallpaper, four fabrics coordinate, one in a solid color and the rest patterned. This multi-pattern interplay works wonderfully because of the color connection, offset by a solid, textured floor and monochrome sofa.

The periwinkle blue sofa and matching pillow are covered in a diamond-dot, textured cotton blend fabric. The casual, tie-top cotton panels have a golden yellow background sprinkled with floral bouquets in rosy reds, warm and cool greens and periwinkle/aqua blues. Close-ups of these flower groupings are framed on two of the sofa pillows.

One chair and another pillow sport a moiré plaid print that mixes up the blues and yellows with dominant greens, calling further attention to this third color family. The other chair and matching ottoman wear an additional pattern, a pretty, blue and white check accented by tiny, yellow and green flower buds.

*S*oaring ceilings give this great room an airy feel, but this cozy conversational grouping warms up a beckoning corner. The mood is most definitely warm here, with a generous mix of golds, burnished reds and terra-cotta, accented with temperature-bridging green.

Hung casually from wooden rings, the simple drapes are made of two perfectly coordinated, cotton and cotton-blend fabrics. Against a textured, neutral ground, the generously sized citrus pattern works well in the large room, lined and cuffed with a charming plaid.

Texture plays a part in the comfortable feel of this space, starting with the sofa and its variety of pillows. The bold stripes, which echo the colors in the plaid curtain fabric, include tiny, raised outlines. Each pillow is made from one or two textured fabrics enhanced by luxurious trims.

The facing chair is upholstered in two fabrics, a soft, chenille paisley outlined by a cinnamon-red solid. Notice how well the warm, caramel-colored wood in this inviting room blends with the fabric palette.

Care to sit down?

Classic red, white and blue cotton fabrics set a breezy mood in this casual family room, a comfortable spot for the gang to gather for television watching and games. Four coordinating prints are used here, each carefully placed for optimal mix and match effect. The ticking-striped slipcover is durable and washable, very important factors in a well-lived room. Its small-scale, blue ticking pattern provides a subtle anchor for the bolder accent fabrics. The tab-top panels framing the window sport a blue and white stripe and the multi-plaid pillows and ottoman infuse the scheme with a bright dose of red. This color is also picked up in a fabric-covered frame on the end table. Accent pillows are made of all three fabrics, in addition to a fourth provençal blue print with red and white accents. Some of the pillows sport two fabrics, accentuating the coordinated pattern interplay in the room.

Bedrooms

Photos courtesy of Calico Corners

Photo courtesy of Calico Corners

*T*rue toile lovers often want to surround themselves with the classic pictorial fabric, as seen in this breathtaking bedroom. The flowery toile covers wall panels, the headboard and a bedside footstool in addition to the dust ruffle, duvet cover and several pillows.

A lively, blue and white gingham adds contrast and contributes to the cheerful mood. A row of oversized buttons charmingly "connects" the second fabric to the bottom of the bed cover, and checks also edge the duvet, cover two large shams and accent two other pillows.

Cool blue offers a calming component to this room, as does the solid neutral floor and white-painted wood. For the ultimate toile enthusiast, it's a dream come true.

This sitting room adjoins the toile bedroom on the previous page. Here, another toile is used to frame French doors, and a windowpane check on the chair and ottoman adds continuity to the theme. The curtains introduce bright yellow into the mix, but the connection between the rooms is readily apparent.

Edged with blue cording, the Sheffield valance shows off medallion motifs in this toile. Note that the drapery tie-backs and lining are made from the same smaller check as in the bedroom. The pillow on the chair picks up the toile, framed with a blue fringe.

About Toile

Marie Antoinette's legendary love for toile (pronounced "twal") is said to have originally spurred the popularity of this unique, versatile fabric. Looking at these gorgeous, pictorial prints, it's no wonder that storybook toile is still a decorating favorite today. Named for a town near Versailles, "Toile de Juoy" patterns were originally limited to red or blue etchings on a cream ground. Today's toiles come in a variety of beautiful colors, including reverse whites on dark solids. Printed on soft cotton, toiles depict idyllic country living scenes, historical and mythological vignettes and flowery nature cameos, each telling its own timeless tale. Used in abundance, this fabric is perfect for Country French and antique lovers, and works as an accent in almost any setting. Toile cut-outs can turn pillows and seat cushions into small works of art—and stimulating conversation pieces!

The key to the beauty of this bedroom retreat is balance, the combination of neutral flooring and walls and a mix of richly colored cottons in patterned prints.

The palette blends red and blue accented by gold and green, yet the darkened, muted qualities make for a restful room. The vividly detailed, ethnic inspired pattern is used generously around the room, starting with the casually-hung curtains and the pillows in the sitting area.

The fabric drapes a bedside table, covers a collection of pillow shams and makes a surprise appearance as a red-trimmed accessory for the bamboo blinds.

The tiny check on the sofa reads as a deep red solid, matching more bed pillows and one side of the reversible quilt. A third, striped fabric brings in more blue, gold and green on pillows and the dust ruffle, and a cleverly designed center pillow compliments with tri-colored trim.

Looking at the coordinating accessories in this room, it's clear no detail was overlooked.

Eight different fabrics are used in this bedroom, yet you'd never call it a "busy" space. Why? The largest piece, the bed, is covered in ultra-neutral white, and the drapery fabrics also feature neutral and solid color materials.

The pattern mix, in a color scheme of muted red, white and blue, is displayed in the array of delightful accent pillows and the curtain cuff. Note the creative use of dual fabrics in the ruffle-trimmed envelope and small rectangular pillows. Neutral wall paint helps maintain a calm mood in this bedroom, yet it's a textile-lover's paradise.

This bedroom also starts with a white duvet cover, the perfect canvas from which to launch a palette of vivacious primary colors. This room for a sporty teen combines ruffles and florals alongside strong solids and stripes.

The royal blue curtains are brightened with bands of a yellow, blue and white dot-floral fabric, and this combination is reversed on the dust ruffle and bolster pillow. The shams and an accent pillow show off a red and gold floral print, trimmed with more blue.

A bench cushion is covered in a flecked white material with blue stripes matching another accent pillow. Paint, wallpaper and art carry out the theme to complete this beautifully coordinated room.

Cascading gathers surround this fleur de lis bedspread in a teen's room, combined with the dust ruffle for a pretty "double flounce" effect. The burgundy fabric is accented by the ecru, eyelet-stripe flounce and the coordinating striped dust ruffle underneath. This double theme is also carried out in the two rows of ruffles edging the matching pillow shams.

The surprise of a paisley-print on the front shams works wonderfully because the pattern is so color coordinated, picking up the bedspread shade and incorporating rich gold to match the back sham ruffles. The open-ended shams are accented with the striped fabric as well as burgundy trim and tie-up laces.

The welting around the edge of the bedspread is covered with the striped fabric, completing a very well thought out ensemble.

Stenciled wallpaper border, unique drawer pulls and other accessories pay homage to man's best friend in this charming bedroom for a child. The bed fabrics certainly add to the fun with a bright mix of stripes, checks and a novelty stamp-pattern.

The knife-edge pillow features a white paisley print on a blue ground with red, button-topped corners. The cute box pillow and matching comforter seem to be covered by a pet's red pawprints, actually hand-stamped onto the white fabric.

The other pillows add to the red, white and blue color scheme, each bold print playing off the other for a "more the merrier" combination.

Small areas of intense color play peekaboo with subtle/neutral tones on walls, flooring and bed cover in this delightful girl's room. Charming touches on the bedding include patchwork pockets to hold secret notes and other treasures.

Zippy rickrack trims the white bed cover, which features cleverly pinched corners embellished with sweet bows. The red rickrack also decorates ruffled pillow shams and a centerpiece pocket pillow. This pillow holds stuffed animals, which are also hung on nearby wall pegs and depicted in the framed print.

The wallpaper border catches the multi-color scheme, emphasizing blue in the subtly striped dust ruffle and two bright, star-print pillows.

This little girl's room features boldly painted walls in a coral, green and white princess theme. In matching colors, a subtle dot print on the fitted bedspread compliments the brazen stripes. Whispery-sheer fabric cascades from a crown fashioned of gold painted mat board. The sheer panels with casing top slide onto a canopy frame, which was wall-mounted. Lace delicately trims the quilted bed cover and shams creating a feminine room fit for a special princess.

Accent pillows introduce two color-coordinating star fabrics, along with another novelty print and the same solid coral seen on the dust ruffle These pillows include more lace along with white ball fringe. The princess's infamous frog sits atop a clever centerpiece pillow.

Here's another western motif for big brother, this one in a quieter, mostly neutral palette. The bedspread's retro cowboy-themed pattern is a subtle white with taupe hues. Wallpaper and accent pillows add additional color to the scheme.

A focal point is the character pillow, which is framed with a coordinating taupe fabric and fringed with a luxurious surprise—suede.

This boy's room is decorated around a key item, the western pictorial rug, which inspires a palette of red, blue and off-white. The clever banner valance decorating the shutters is a noteworthy addition, with silver "sheriff's badges" emphasizing the theme.

The bedding includes a solid blue, fitted comforter and a pleated dust ruffle in a western-motif fabric. Pillows match both of the fabrics, the wallpaper coordinates, and all work perfectly with the fun and colorful rug.

This nursery forgoes typical baby pastels and bright primary colors, emphasizing a nature-loving palette of neutrals and soft green. The zebra rug suggested the jungle theme, carried through in a wallpaper border, artwork and pillows.

White walls blend with the sheer curtains, accented with decorative threads running through the fabric. White is also the color of the crib comforter and box pillow cushion on the rocker, the latter edged with earthy red to match the carpet.

The pillows pick up the green of the dust ruffle and natural golden-tan tones. (Don't forget to remove the pillows when baby is sleeping.) One features a hand-painted, storybook giraffe and another is covered in a faux basket weave print.

Dining Areas

Photos courtesy of Calico Corners

$\mathcal{S}$ophisticated neutrals lend a touch of class that's perfect for a formal dining room. Each of the three silky fabrics used here will gleam in the reflected light of the chandelier or burning candles.

The glamorous damask tablecloth is woven with metallic gold and finished with a generous metallic fringe. The cartridge-pleated drapes are understated, yet elegant in a rich, shiny gold.

The checked slipper chairs pick up the golden scheme and add contemporary black and dark gray, the latter shade matching the paint of the walls. The rug contains all of these colors, for a perfectly coordinated, elegant dining room.

When the dining room adjoins the kitchen, tie the two rooms together with matching fabrics on the bar stools and windows. This pretty, burgundy and gold floral covers kitchen stool pads and decorates a nearby window top.

This informal eating area demonstrates a clever way to cover inexpensive bar stools and create a tie-in with breakfast table chairs. The bright fruit-print fabric unifies the unmatched seating in the room, disguising the stools from seat to floor with a cheerful covering. A subtle beige and white check combines with the vibrant pattern, seemingly held together by fabric strips and oversized buttons. A double-thick row of cotton brush trim circles the stool seats, adding further interest to these charming, fabric-inspired accessories.

Black and white is always an energetic combination, just right for a pick-me-up in the breakfast area/kitchen. This window is treated with cafe curtains and a valance made with three coordinating black and white fabrics. The windowpane check and mini-floral prints are also used to make eye-opening cups to top the valance.

The black and white theme is carried out on linens for the breakfast bar, with flowered place mats accented by checked napkins. (No fabric need be wasted here!) Solid black and white napkin rings, checked dishes and tiny flower pots show some of the many possible ways to accessorize this motif.

Hint

For an aromatic surprise, use the place mat instructions (reduced in size) to make a fabric trivet. Add ground cinnamon to the batting and when a warm teapot is resting on the trivet, a delicious scent will permeate the room.

Cushions make outdoor furniture so much more comfortable, encouraging sunset watchers to linger into a warm, summer evening. These seat and chair-back cushions are covered in acrylic, an ideal outdoor fabric because it's durable, easy to clean and resists fading and mildew. Cotton canvas, muslin and plasticized cottons are also good choices for the patio or deck.

Here, cotton accent pillows include a floral print and a Victorian beach scene. Crisp, seaside blue and white is the color scheme, with green and rose used as accents. The cushions are made with generous ties, leaving colorful bows and streamers to dance in the breeze.

Pillows

*R*ich fabrics combine, pulling a bedroom scheme together to a focal point grouping. Three ruffled, striped shams mix with two others made from exotic print fabric, the latter trimmed with fringe. Two other accent pillows pick up the fabric on the sofa. The centerpiece pillow in silky beige calls attention to the bits of gold scattered around the room, then incorporates red, blue and white in attached cording and four-corner tassels.

*S*ix fabrics work together to complete this picture perfect look. The shams are double-ruffled, using the bedspread's eyelet flounce and a new gold plaid. On the small pillow, the primary fabric is framed with more eyelet and a solid burgundy, with matching braid trim. This same trim and solid fabric work on the open-ended paisley/stripe pillow shams, tied up with burgundy laces.

elveteen and cotton/linen mix it up on these accent pillows, featuring a palette of greens, pinks and neutrals. The two striped velveteen pillows are dressed with gold buttons, studding attached strips of solid green velveteen to match the other pillow. The upper corners are adorned with pink tassels. In front, a lush floral pillow displays ruffled edges.

Hint

Easy ways to adorn pillows -
wrap with beautiful ribbons, sew tassels to corners, embellish with antique buttons, tack on vintage doilies or handkerchiefs, pin on antique jewelry, edge with beaded trim.

This eclectic mix of pillows combines six different fabric patterns. The round, box-type pillow is the centerpiece, hand-stamped with paw prints to accent the room's pet theme. The pillow's piping is covered by the subtle red pattern that frames the striped shams. Topped with buttons, this print also accents the corners of the blue print pillow. Checks and stars and stripes add to this whimsical and colorful scheme.

Knife-edge star-pattern pillows complete the multi-color mix in this bedroom. The shams and centerpiece pillows are ruffled and accented with a row of bright red rickrack. The clever patchwork pocket holds the bedtime companion of a little girl's choice.

A masterfully coordinated pillow cluster is created to accessorize a teen's bright and cheerful room. The shams on the back of the bed are ruffled and trimmed with blue welting. This blue also ruffles the matching accent pillow and details the bolster. The striped pillow sports a generous ruffle as well.

V ibrant, animated fabric prints combine for playful girl's bed accessories. A solid coral and star-print pillow share a lace trim, as do the shams, picking up the look of the bedspread. This star print frames another novelty fabric in the front pillow, which is accented with white ball fringe. The coordinating star fabric is also edged with cottony balls.

The colorful plaid pillows in this casual room are accessorized with an extra-long, bullion fringe made of soft cotton. The ticking pillows are edged in dark blue bands to coordinate with the curtain fabric. Blue tabs also button up two coordinating prints on the far left pillow.

Several different pillow designs and fabrics combine for this interesting grouping, with coordinated color tying them together. The striped shams are flanged, then ruffled at the corners. This fabric combines with a paisley for a small, rectangular pillow, trimmed with fringe. Knife-edge, blue-striped pillows also share this fringe.

The corners of the Indian floral print pillow are accented with dark blue, then topped with red buttons. The solid, envelope pillow is trimmed with an additional red and white print, and a plaid pillow in similar colors sits nearby.

Window Coverings

*S*assy blue and white stripes create a cheerful kitchen window valance accessorized with playful hook covers. The retro, coffee pot cut-outs also add a splash of red to the otherwise all-white kitchen. The window panels in the adjoining family room carry on the bold color scheme with coordinating blue and white stripes.

The spirit of fun is evident in this family recreation room. The brightly striped roman valance likely celebrates the colors of a favorite sports team, because the fabric is held in place with clever, baseball-covered hooks. It's not difficult to achieve this eye-catching look. The hooks are made with real balls glued onto cut pieces of dowel.

Hint

Use your imagination when thinking of innovative items to use for hanging valances or curtains, such as:
- *An antique oar*
- *Long wooden strips of pegs*
- *Antique or ornate metal coat hooks*
- *Door knobs*
- *Drawer pulls*

*H*ere's an interesting twist on a flounce-top valance. The tie-tabs on these wispy, striped sheers are not formed into bows, but knotted and left to cascade loosely from the rod. The valance offers a lighter take on traditional balloon shades, with portions of the gold and white fabric lifted to create a billowy, scalloped look. It's easy to create with shirring tape. This attractive valance is topped with a lovely, smocked header.

A striped awning valance dispenses with fuss and frills, yet gives a jaunty air to this game room, where friends gather to play pool. Fringed with a gold brush trim, the fabric is reminiscent of an old time pub, contributing to jovial atmosphere. This window treatment is easy to make using curtain rods in two different sizes.

The patterned fabric on this easy, rod pocket valance matches the stars and stripes pillow on the bed on page 33. Note the clever rod decoration here, a wooden bone to match the doggie-themed drawer pulls and wallpaper border.

This colorful valance matches the bed in the charming room featured on page 34. It displays the same bright, patchwork pockets, also spiced up with the red rickrack trim. These pockets might also hold small toys, or perhaps, her most secret letters.

These "curtains" are hung on a pulley-style clothesline for a whimsical laundry room valance. Clothespins add to the fun, holding an either/or pattern of solid and checked dishtowels. Use your imagination and sew up a mix of fabrics to hang, including denim with pockets, "patched" solids, etc.

Hint

Other whimsical valance ideas:
• *In a child's room, hang doll clothes from close pins on ropes spanning the windows.*
• *College team pennants*
• *Antique linens such as tea towels or small tablecloths*
• *Vintage handkerchiefs*

This masculine, rust and green study is enhanced by simple, tab-top drapes in a blend of solid and plaid fabrics. Dark green borders the plaid on all four sides of each panel, which hangs from a wooden rod with the help of deep rust tabs. Rather than tying, the tabs attach with large, wooden buttons. It's a look that's very buttoned-up, just the way he likes.

Hint

For a quicker, easier construction, use iron-on hemming tape to add the borders to this type of drapery panel.

$\mathscr{H}$ere's a unique idea that's in keeping with the increasingly popular slouchy look for casual curtains. (These are definitely not your mother's tailored draperies!) In a green and gold plaid with sienna accents, these curtains hang loosely and also sport a distinctive smocked appearance. Shirring tape helps gather the upper material so that it falls into loose, ruffly bunches.

Hint

Iron-on shirring tape makes fast work of complicated looking effects like this.

he neutral cream color of this patterned sheer would allow it to fit into most any decor. The clever use of carved, wooden Indian hooks lend an exotic feel to the gauzy fabric, where more formal hardware would set a different mood. The top ends of the fixed panel are each tied to a hook, letting the panel drape casually in the center. Then a graceful swag is added for an elegant, finished look.

This butterscotch fabric is unusual, topping a sheer ecru ground with soft, chenille stripes. The flip valance combined with box pleats adds an interesting detail to the classic drapery. Note how the rod is hung just below the ceiling, creating an illusion of height in the room. With one on either side of the window, these fixed panels offer a lovely frame in a fabric that's irresistible to the touch.

These paisley drapes go with the bedroom pictured on page 28. The fabric is the same used for pillow shams on the bed, while the drapery cuff, fashioned of burgundy fabric, also trims an accent pillow. A black, wrought-iron rod and matching rings helps to bring out the rich hues in these fabrics.

This curtain panel matches the valance on page 57. Both the valance and curtain sport a gathered cuff on top. The filmy, sheer material keeps the look very casual and airy. Note the coordinating damask wallpaper, contributing to an aura of romance.

*A*n the popular slouchy style, this white-on-white, woven print panel is ultra casual, yet nothing short of beautiful. Attached loops hang the sheer, textured fabric from a three-hook wall detail—a creative solution for a fixed panel. Originally meant to hold hats or coats, this carved wooden piece does the new job well, and with interest!

*H*int

The best types of fabric to use for this slouchy effect, would be soft, thin materials such as voiles, sheers, silks, rayons, chiffons and even some lace fabrics. When visiting your fabric store, unroll a length of fabric from the bolt and hold it up to see how it drapes. If the fabric is too stiff or heavy, it won't drape nicely and this effect will not be created.

his curtain is made from an intriguing fabric, creating a neutral accessory that also becomes a focal point. Pieces of white and green threads are interwoven into the wispy-sheer material, the ends left to dangle for a textured accent. The slim tie tops are made of coordinating green fabric, and tied into large bows beneath the wooden rod. (See nursery on page 38)

Tablecloths

You've covered your windows with curtains and drapes, added pillows to couches and chairs, and made bedcovers and dust ruffles galore. Now it's time to breathe fresh life into empty corners and bare spaces in your house. What better way to accent a room's decor, than covering small tables with more pretty fabrics and adding them to your beautifully decorated rooms.

Think of a round side table as an opportunity to show off more decorative fabric in your room. Atop a floor-length table skirt, there are many different ways to layer a second print for a beautifully coordinated look.

The floral topper and coordinating check underskirt (above) matches a nearby bedcover. The topper is gathered up into sections with shirring tape to create a pretty, scalloped effect

The elegant table at left, incorporates two interesting fabrics embellished with trim. The gold skirt is edged in dark blue cord and the lovely paisley topper boasts a matching blue fringe. This table beautifully accessorizes a corner of the room, adding color, soft lighting and a bit of greenery.

Living Room

This before and after story depicts the transformation of a brand new condominium into a comfortable, inviting vacation home. The photographs in this section show the way each room looked at the close of escrow, then reveal the end results after paint, furniture, fabric and accessories were added.

Of course, textiles get top billing in this book, and each of the sewing projects shown here are easy to replicate. Instructions are provided beginning on page 92. Even if your sewing experience is quite limited, you'll be surprised at what you can accomplish!

At first purchase, this modest, two-bedroom dwelling was a blank slate, with white walls, beige carpeting, no window treatments and—because it is a second home—no furniture coming off of a moving van.

The owners were thrilled with the prospects of a summer retreat near the California shore, but before they could begin to enjoy it, they were faced with an immediate task—decorating. The budget was limited, but a sewing machine stood ready, and several hand-me-downs had been made available.

First, a sofa and several pieces of 1970s-era maple furniture were donated, including a dining set, coffee and end table and some nightstands. The sofa's soft blue and white color scheme seemed a good fit for the beach, but the maple furniture definitely didn't. So, the first job was to paint all the wooden pieces white, then sand the dry paint to achieve a slightly distressed, "beach cottage" finish.

Much of the furniture would be used in the living room. Using the blue and white plaid sofa as a key, paint and several fabrics were selected to transform this cold, empty space (pictured in its original state on these pages) into the cozy room on the following page.

The classic combination of soothing blue and fresh white give the front room a breezy, relaxing feel, just the right ambience for a vacation getaway at the shore. The walls were painted a sea-going blue, with a darker blue tone used for the inside of an archway leading to the dining room. A pretty, checked fabric frames the sliding glass doors with rod pocket panels, accented with a centerpiece valance in a blue on white stripe. Pillows were covered with a smaller check print, as well as a floral material that adds touches of pink and green to the palette.

This stairway window is visible from the living room, so the same fabrics were used here for the roll-up shade. The check is lined with the floral fabric for a two-tone effect when the shade is raised. Contrasting bands were made out of the striped valance material, then topped with floral-covered buttons. (Velcro® dots make this shade easy to raise and lower.)

Painted wooden starfish add a creative touch and help anchor the color scheme and tie it in with the dining room. Note the addition of the architectural detail above the window to add decorative interest.

This wicker chair was a $10 garage sale find, yet it looks nearly new with a freshly covered cushion and accent pillows. The floral print in the seat cushion provides a pretty contrast to the assorted checked fabrics. The front pillows here are reversible, one side matching the curtains and the other overed in a smaller check. The two background pillows were purchased, as was the mirror, which reflects the complimentary yellow color in the adjacent dining room.

ike the rest of this condominium, the kitchen offered a neutral base with white ceramic tile and a beige floor. The dining room boasted a second fireplace with a white mantel. More white-painted maple furniture would be used here, and the blue and white color scheme would be continued into these rooms, this time accenting a dominant yellow. This complimentary color was chosen to balance the cool palette, and because the owners love a warm, sunny kitchen and eating area. A medium-intensity yellow paint was selected along with three decorator fabrics, a white/yellow/blue toile, a blue and white floral print and a windowpane plaid with blue stripes on a yellow and white ground.

n the living room antique Mexican tiles were applied to the fireplace, adding another coordinating blue and white pattern to the mix. Also, note the arrangement of white candle holders with blue candles and other accessories. The two-toned archway is visible here, leading to the yellow dining room and kitchen.

aint and fabrics certainly did warm up the informal dining room, now a welcoming place for meals and conversation. The sliding glass door and picture window were both accented with lovely toile drapes, the simple panels attaching to white rods with rings. A swag was made for the window out of coordinating plaid, lined with blue and white print fabric. Then, seat cushions were covered, two in plaid and two in toile to match the window treatment. The chandelier lampshades were also covered with fabric, picking up the toile print.

he owners' collection of blue and white china, including Chinese porcelain, blue willow and Spode, work perfectly in this room. The yellow paint brings out the beautiful blue color of the pieces, which are displayed on the mantel, hutch and dining table. Some of the plates are also hung in the kitchen, shown on the following page.

The master bedroom is upstairs, completely removed from the main living area, so an entirely different color scheme was selected for this room. A set of slipper chairs in a beige brocade fabric became the starting point for the color palette. An inexpensive brass bedstead was found at a flea market and transformed into an "upscale" decorator item when it was "rusted" using a faux finish kit. This dark red color was also used as a key.

A muted, dark intensity palette of red, green and golden beige was chosen for the bedroom's fabrics, in a mix of floral, striped and checked prints. It was decided that the walls would remain white, a neutral expanse to contrast with the strong pattern mix. The owners enjoy the feeling of a bedroom retreat and decided to do something special with this room's recessed window alcove. Turn the page to see the new look.

alk about a sunny kitchen! The bright squares of yellow in the curtain fabric take on the glow of the sun as it begins to set over the ocean. Matching the dining room swag, the gathered valance and cafe curtains help unify the two open rooms. Note the charming use of blue grosgrain ribbon tabs, accented with yellow buttons, to attach the curtains to a tension rod.

The artwork on the wall was framed and matted to blend in with the color scheme. Note how the green and pink of the calla lilies add pleasing accent notes.

Cozy and comfortable to be sure, this room is awash in beautiful color and delightful pattern interplay. First, the bedding is a focal point, with the richly-hued floral duvet cover accented by a small check at the lower end and a striped dust ruffle. Note the oversized buttons covered in floral fabric, a creative accent atop the duvet's checked panel. A sheer, tulle canopy adds drama and frames a collection of pillows in a variety of color-coordinating patterns.

The medium-scale striped fabric was also made into rod-pocket curtains to cover the alcove window, as well as a valance for the bedside window. Curtain panels surrounding all sides of the alcove create a cozy backdrop for the chairs.

*L*ining all sides of the recessed alcove, these curtains envelop the chairs and table, creating the feeling of a separate sitting area in the bedroom. This cozy spot is a perfect place to relax and enjoy coffee and the Sunday paper.

*R*ather than use this small window as a light source, the condo owners opted to play up its long, narrow shape and create a decorative accent for the bedroom. It was covered with a stationary shade, using tension rods at both the top and bottom. The shade was made from a narrow-striped, red and beige fabric, then accented with a tasseled banner valance in the bolder stripe.

To add extra interest, a purchased wooden shelf was painted red and mounted above the window, then covered in silk ivy. Did you notice the lamp bases in the room were also painted red?

Children's Room

The second bedroom would be used as a child's room, occasionally to accommodate visiting adult guests as well. A bright, cheerful color scheme was in order, something that would delight the youngster without being too juvenile for older folk. In keeping with the coastal location, a nautical/patriotic red, white and blue theme was chosen for this room.

The walls would remain white, leaving room for lots of bold red and blue patterns for window treatments, etc. First, a patchwork print was selected, offering a vibrant combination of "pieced" squares in star, stripe, solid and check patterns. Then, a starred blue and white print and red gingham check were added to the mix. Solid blue twin comforters and shams were purchased for the room, and then it was time to get sewing!

This room is definitely colorful and fun, without being too heavy-handed. The use of fabric is well thought out, allowing blue and white to dominate the room amidst scattered touches of bright red. The multi-patchwork fabric was used as a topper for a star-print tablecloth and to cover foam (easy to make) cornices for the windows. Small stars also accent a tiny lampshade and form drapes, which are tied back with nautical cords. Reversible bed and chair pillows, in simple knife-edge style, were made out of the star fabric and red gingham. The starry motif was enhanced with a hand-stamped border that runs all the way around the room. To complete this look, a chenille flag accent pillow was purchased, along with nautical-themed artwork.

The second window in the child's room was covered with a roll-up shade in the star print and topped with another bright cornice. The shade is detailed with white cording, tied in nautical-style knots to hold it partially aloft. This clever window treatment is surprisingly easy to make.

his corner table pairs a blue and white star-print skirt with a square, patchwork topper in red, white and blue to match the bedroom's window treatments. The table offers an interesting space for extra lighting and to showcase beach-oriented decor. The topper was easy to make utilizing a fabric that was purchased already pieced!

ecause it's attached to the child's room, this bathroom carries on the same decorative theme. Atop a purchased shower curtain, the rod-pocket valance is made of the red and white gingham used for accent pillows in the bedroom. Lighthouse-themed artwork and accent pieces keep the mood nautical.

Instructions

Table Coverings

Many types of fabric work well to create lovely tablecloths and toppers. For a round tablecloth, you'll want a fabric that drapes well. If you'd like a layered look, you might want to mix a striped tablecloth with a floral or a plaid with a stripe. Coordinate the fabrics for your tablecloth and topper with the colors in your room.

Round Tablecloth (examples, page 68)

Supplies Needed
Fabric
Large piece of butcher, newsprint or craft paper
String
Pencil
Pins
Scissors
Measuring tape and yard stick

1. Measure diameter of table. (A)

2. Measure from top of table to floor (the drop).(B) If making a topper, measure from top of table to the desired drop. (C)

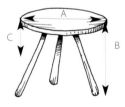

The size of the skirt is the diameter of the table, plus twice the drop length, plus a 1" hem allowance for a floor length skirt.

3. To determine the required width for your project, you will need to sew panels of your fabric together. If you're using a print fabric that requires matching, you will probably need to purchase additional fabric. Use the formula below to figure how much fabric you'll need:

For solid fabric

Skirt size ÷ fabric width = number of panels (round up to nearest whole number)

Skirt size x number of panels = total inches

Total inches ÷ 36 = total yardage.

For printed fabric

Skirt size ÷ vertical design repeat = number of repeats in each panel

Vertical design repeat x number of repeats in each panel = length of panels

Skirt size ÷ fabric width = number of panels

Length of panels x number of panels = inches

Inches ÷ 36 = total yardage

When sewing the panels together for your tablecloth, seams should be placed at sides rather than the center. When sewing two fabric panels for a skirt or topper, you'll need to use a full width of fabric at the center with a half-width sewn to each side. (When sewing three full fabric panels, you'll need to use a full width of fabric at the center with a full width sewn to each side.)

4. Cut the fabric and sew the pieces together according to figure B with a $\frac{5}{8}$" seam allowance. You will then have a big square of fabric.

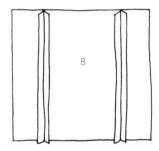

5. Fold the square of fabric into quarters.

6. For a pattern, cut a square of paper the same size as the folded fabric. Place pattern on folded fabric so corner A is on top of fabric corner A. Take a piece of string and tie one end around a pin and the other end around a pencil; the distance between the pin and pencil should equal the radius of the tablecloth. Put the pin at corner A of paper holding pen at right angles; draw an arc from B to C. Cut along the traced line of pattern from C to B.

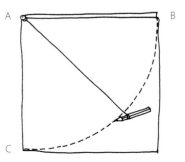

7. Fold raw edge under $1/2$" and press. Turn under $1/2$" again. Press and stitch.

Square Table Topper (example page 90)

1. For square topper, cut square piece of fabric large enough that the corners extend approximately one third of the way to the floor.

2. For hem, turn raw edges of topper under $1/2$"; press. Turn under $1/2$" again and sew in place.

3. Add embellishments as desired, such as fringe, cords or tassels.

Pillows

Making your own pillows is an ideal way to add color, interest and drama to your home. You will see various pillows sprinkled throughout this book. There are instructions for the most popular pillows—knife edge, knife edge with envelope opening, turkish, ruffled, flange, boxed and bolster. You might want to vary your pillows with the addition of trims, tassels, ribbon, rickrack, stamps, etc.

Of course there are many other pillow styles you might want to try. See Leisure Arts, *The Ultimate Pillow Book* for additional pillow styles and more instructions.

Let your imagination go when selecting fabrics. This is the fun part of creating unique pillows. You can be guided by your present furnishings and accessories with regard to color, trim and special embellishments.

For pillows that will receive heavy use, choose a firm, woven fabric that will keep its shape.

For decorative pillows, choose loose weaves for texture and interest.

For durability, select firm, woven, synthetics or blends that will last longer.

For outdoor cushions, you'll want fade resistant, easy-care fabrics (light-colored solids are most fade resistant).

Natural fabrics (cotton, linen, silk, wool) are easy to work with, comfortable, feel good, wear well and retain their shape. But they will shrink, wrinkle and fade.

Synthetic fabrics (acetate, acrylic, nylon, polyester, rayon) are durable, easy-care, washable, retain shape, and are wrinkle-free. But they're not as easy to handle and can be uncomfortable.

A good choice is a cotton and polyester blend which has the qualities of both fabric types.

Colors and patterns are up to you. Select fabrics that will coordinate with your total scheme.

Shop at fabric stores, fabric departments of discount chains, or upholstery shops. Look for vintage fabrics and accessories at flea markets, auctions, antique shops or garage sales.

More fabric facts

Choose fabrics with a straight grain (cross wise threads running perpendicular to lengthwise threads). Don't use printed fabric that is off-grain or the pillow will appear crooked.

Pillow Forms:

Pillow forms come in a wide variety of shapes and sizes. Despite the variety available, there will be times when you want something different. In this case, you'll need to make your own.

Making your own pillow form

You can use muslin or a plain, lightweight fabric for a covering. Remember to cut your pillow form fabric slightly smaller than your finished pillow. Make a paper pattern in the shape desired. Pin the pattern to two pieces of your fabric. Cut the fabric and sew the pillow form in the desired shape leaving an opening for filling. (See instructions for knife edge pillow page 94).

Stuff with either cotton batting or polyester fiberfill to the preferred plumpness. Hand stitch the opening closed.

To make a smooth pillow

Take a fist-size wad of filling and gently pull it apart to fluff and separate the fibers. Use a crochet hook or chop stick to stuff filling into the corners. Or wrap a layer of batting around a pillow form and insert in the pillow.

Other fillings for pillow forms:

Kapok – decorators and upholsterers prefer kapok which fills pillows softly and completely.

Down – the ultimate filling. However, it's expensive and hard to handle. If you really want to have a pillow form of down, have an upholsterer make one for you.

Getting Started:

First you'll need to know how much fabric to buy for your pillow. Consult the chart below for yardage required according to the size pillow form you'll be using:

	45" wide	54" wide
12" square	$1/2$ yd.	$1/2$ yd.
14" square	$1/2$ yd.	$1/2$ yd.
16" square	$1/2$ yd.	$1/2$ yd.
18" square	$5/8$ yd.	$5/8$ yd.
20" square	$5/8$ yd.	$5/8$ yd.
24" square	$1 1/2$ yd.	$3/4$ yd.
30" square	2 yds.	$1 3/4$ yd.

Pillow Closures

There are several ways to close a pillow. The choice is dependent on the type of pillow and how much use it will receive.

If you don't plan to wash the pillow, you can close the seam with hand stitching after the pillow form is inserted.

Another way to close a pillow is with an overlap closure (sometimes called an envelope closure, see instructions this page). This is an easier method than adding a zipper and you'll still be able to remove the pillow form for laundering. Adding a Velcro® strip to the overlap creates a neat, secure closure. If adding a zipper to your pillow, follow the instructions on the package for best results.

Knife Edge Pillow (example page 74)

1. Cut two pieces of fabric $1/2$" larger all around, than your pillow form.

2. Place the two pieces of fabric right sides together and pin.

3. Stitch around all sides with a $1/2$" seam allowance leaving an opening on one side for pillow form.

4. Press seams open, trim corners, turn pillow right side out.

5. Insert pillow form in opening, then hand stitch opening closed.

If you wish to make a round pillow, follow the same instructions, but before turning, clip the curves of the seam allowance.

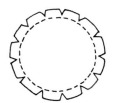

Knife Edge Pillow with Envelope Opening

This type of pillow is made for ease of laundering

Cut fabric

Form size	Front	Back (2 pieces)
12" square	13" x 13"	10" x 13"
14" square	15"x15"	11" x 15"
16" square	17" x 17"	12" x 17"
18" square	19" x 19"	13" x 19"

1. For an 18" square pillow, cut one piece of fabric 19" x 19" and two pieces 13" x 19" (or use sizes from above). On the wrong side of the two 13" x 19" pieces, turn in a $1/2$" hem on one of the long ends. Press. Turn in another $1/2$" and press, pin and machine stitch close to edge.

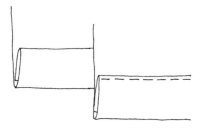

2. Remove pins. With right side facing up and hemmed edges on the inside, overlap the two back pieces so that they create one 19" x 19" piece.

3. Pin together along hemmed edges. Pin front to back, right sides together. Sew a $1/2$" seam allowance all around.

 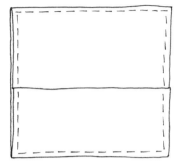

4. Trim corners, remove pins. Turn right side out and insert pillow form.

Turkish Pillow (example page 72)

1. Follow Steps 1 - 3 for knife edge pillow (page 94).

2. After sewing seams, mark a line across each corner as pictured.

3. Tie corners tightly with string, then turn right side out.

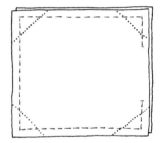 

4. Insert pillow form and hand stitch opening closed.

Ruffled Pillow (example page 49)

1. Cut two pieces of fabric the desired size of your pillow, plus $1/2$" all around.

2. For a 3" ruffle: cut a fabric strip 7" wide, and a length 3 times the diameter of the pillow form + 1". You may have to piece the strips to get the required length.

(For best results, cut the strips across the width of the fabric)

3. Pin the ends of the strips right sides together and sew using $1/2$" seam allowance. Press seams open.

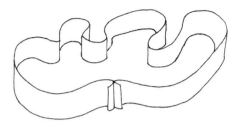

4. Fold the strip in half with wrong sides together, matching the raw edges.

5. Sew a gathering stitch along the raw edge of fabric. Gently pull one end of the bobbin thread holding onto the other end of strip. Adjust the gathers as you go. Once you have gathered it to the correct length, tie a loose knot (or wrap the end of thread around a straight pin), you may want to adjust the gathers later.

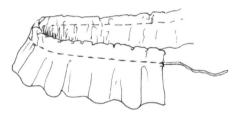

6. Put the ruffle and right side of top piece of pillow together matching raw edges and pin. Stitch ruffle to top piece adjusting fullness of ruffle evenly. For a finished looking pillow, provide extra fullness at the corners.

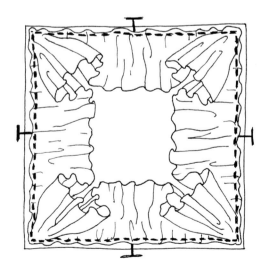

(Continued)

7. Place bottom piece over top piece, right sides together with ruffle in between. Raw edges should be lined up. Stitch a 1/2" seam allowance all the way around pillow. Leave an opening on one side.

8. Turn pillow right side out and insert pillow form. Hand sew opening closed.

Flange Pillow (example page 50)

1. To make a 22" pillow with a 16" form, cut your fabric 22" x 51".

2. On wrong side of fabric at each short end, turn in a 1/4" hem. Press. Turn in another 1/2", press, pin and machine stitch close to edge. Remove pins.

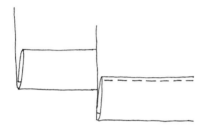

3. Fold fabric in half widthwise, right sides together. Measure 11" on either side of this fold. Fold at this point (at each end) and press.

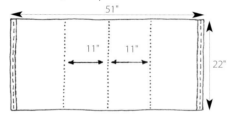

The fabric will overlap in the middle (A).

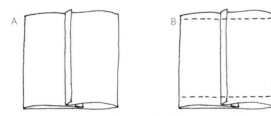

4. Sew up each raw edge with 1/2" seam allowance (B). Trim corners

5. Turn right side out. Top stitch all around, 2 1/2" from the edge. Insert pillow form.

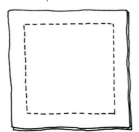

Pillow with Fabric Insert (example page 24)

1. Cut main piece to desired size and then cut center out so that you have a frame. Cut a center piece to desired size but add a seam allowance of 1/2" all around. Cut a back piece the same size as the main piece. You will now have three pieces.

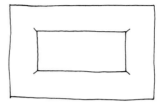

2. Snip into seam allowances at corners of frame on the front piece. Press seam allowance around frame to back.

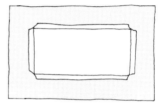

3. Place the center piece behind the frame. Pin in place. Turn to front. Topstitch in place next to folded edge of main piece.

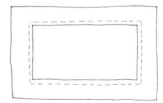

4. Pin front piece to back piece, right sides together and stitch all the way around leaving an opening for pillow form. Trim seams at corners. Turn right side out and press seams. Insert pillow form, then hand sew opening closed.

Rolled or Bolster Pillow (page 31)

1. For fabric amount, measure the circumference (A) of the form, and add 1" for seam allowances. Measure the length (B) of the form, then add 1" for seam allowance.

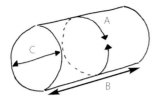

2. Cut a rectangular piece of fabric according to these measurements.

3. Stay stitch in $1/2$" from edge on both short ends.

4. Fold fabric in half lengthwise with right sides facing. Stitch along long edge with $1/2$" seams.

5. To make end sections, measure the end diameter (C) of pillow form and add $1/2$" for seam allowance. Cut out two rounds.

6. Stay stitch $1/2$" in from edge around both round ends.

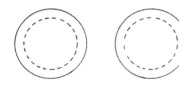

7. Clip both cover and end pieces from edge to stay stitching.

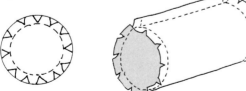

8. Pin the cover piece and one of the end pieces right sides together, raw edges matching. With the end section on top, stitch a $1/2$" seam. Repeat for the other end stitching only half way.

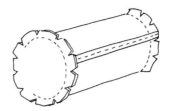

9. Turn the cover right side out and insert the pillow form. Hand stitch the opening closed.

Box-edge Pillow (example page 38)

For square or rectangular pillows.

1. Have foam cut to your desired size (some specialty fabric stores or upholstery studios will cut the foam for you).

2. Measure the width and length of the top of the foam adding $1/2$" to all sides for seam allowances. With these measurements cut the fabric for the front and back.

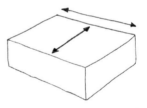

3. For size of boxing strip, measure foam depth and circumference, add $1/2$" to all sides for seam allowances.

If you don't have enough fabric for the strip, you may need to piece it (if so, add 1" to the length of each piece for the seams.) At this point you will add a zipper (if desired) to the boxing strip. Follow the directions on the zipper package.

(Continued)

4. Apply piping if desired. Baste the piping along the $\frac{1}{2}$" seam line on the right side of the front and back pillow pieces. Use a zipper foot with the stitches right next to the piping.

5. Pin the short ends of the boxing strip, right sides together, and stitch with $\frac{1}{2}$" seam allowances.

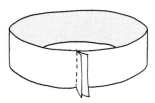

6. Mark the sewn strip in four equal points for square pillow, both top and bottom. For a rectangular pillow, mark corners using the pillow form to measure from. You will want the seam to fall at the center back of the pillow.

7. Stay stitch $\frac{1}{2}$" in from raw edge around top and bottom of boxing strip. Clip to stitching line at each mark.

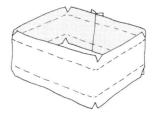

8. Pin the front and the boxing strip right sides together, positioning the clips at the corners. Stitch.

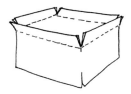

9. Repeat, stitching the back to the other edge of the boxing strip. Leave an opening for inserting the foam.

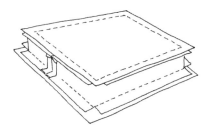

10. Turn cover right side out. Insert foam, hand stitch the opening closed.

If you're going to be using these items in a nursery—you might want to consider adding zippers so that they can be laundered easily.

Window Treatments

Making curtains and draperies can be extremely complicated. But we've tried to take the mystery out of them and make them a littler easier.

We've broken the process down into 8 steps:

1. Choose the treatment (look at magazines, model homes, catalogs, the photographs in this book, etc. to find the look that you like).

2. Choose your fabric

3. Choose hardware

4. Measure windows (see diagram below)

5. Install hardware

6. Figure how much fabric you'll need (page 125)

7. Cut fabric and sew

8. Hang window treatment

It's very important to get correct measurements prior to making your window treatment. Be sure to take all window measurements including an inside and outside mount. You'll want to measure the

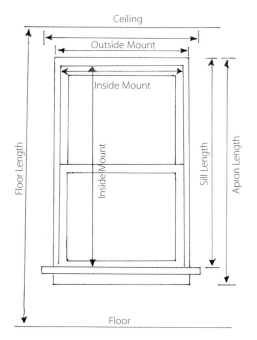

lengths and widths of everything in the window diagram. This way you'll be ready for all possibilities. Measure each window (some windows, even though they look the same, might vary slightly).

Make a drawing or diagram of each of your windows and add the measurements to the diagram. This will be helpful when you go to purchase fabric. The drawing will also be helpful in deciding placement of rods and how long the window treatment should be.

Most decorator fabrics are available in 54" widths, so most of the instructions in this book are figured using 54".

To figure width of treatment:

Multiply the length of the rod or pole by 2 $\frac{1}{2}$ (for fullness). Some window treatments require less fabric (see individual instructions for specific fullness requirements). Add 4" for 1" double side hems.

Rod	Fullness	Side Hems	Width

To figure length of treatment:

Figure the length of treatment (either to sill or floor) and add 8" (for a 4" double hem) and the number of inches for top treatment (see individual instructions for this measurement).

Length	Hem	Top Treatment	Finished length

You'll also have to add the amount of fabric needed for the pocket depending on the type of rod you'll be using. (See Rod Size Chart page 101).

If pattern has a repeat, you'll have to allow for more fabric. Measure the longest part of repeat and add that to the measurement of the length of each fabric piece.

Sometimes you will need to piece your panels because the fabric you are using will not be wide enough. Do not piece down the center; add a narrow piece of fabric to the window frame side of treatment. Use a $\frac{1}{2}$" seam allowance.

After doing all of your measuring, see page 125 to figure the amount of yardage required for your project.

Hemming Window Treatments

Double hems will give your draperies or curtains extra weight. They will hang better and have a more professional look. A 4" double hem is the most common, which means you should add 8" for the bottom hem when calculating yardage. For a 4" double hem, turn bottom of fabric panel 4" to wrong side and press. Turn under 4" again and press. Sew in place by machine or hand. Or you may wish to use iron-on hemming tape.

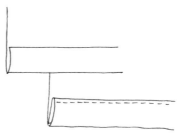

Line panels if desired (see Lining, pages 99-100)

Basic Flat Panels

(Use these panels for all window treatments except those with casings). For treatments with casings see rod pocket curtain instructions (page 101).

1. After measuring and cutting your fabric (and sewing extra widths if necessary), hem sides using a 1" double hem.

2. Make a 4" double hem at bottom of drapes.

3. Construct the header with a 6" double hem.

4. Press and stitch in place.

Easy Lining Method

You will want to line your drapes to screen out heavy sunshine and if you want a finished look to the drapes from the outside.

1. Measure and cut fabrics the same as for basic panels.

2. Lay lining and drape fabrics right sides together on a flat surface. Pin, baste, then machine stitch seams up both sides and along top. Leave hem end open. Clip the corners, then turn right side out and press.

If using light weight fabrics, hem drapes the easy way using iron-on hemming tape.

Basic Lining Method

1. Cut your fabric and lining to the desired cut size of your panels.

2. Trim lining 6" along one selvage and 3" along bottom.

3. Hem the fabric panel and lining fabrics separately. Create a 4" double hem on drapery panel and a 3" double hem on the lining.

4. Place fabric panel and lining right sides together. Pin along one side seam, with top edges even. Bottom edge of the lining is 1" shorter than the fabric panel. Stitch one side seam together. Press seam toward lining.

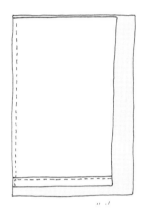

5. Pull the lining over to meet the other side of the fabric panel, right sides will still be together. Pin this side seam together, and stitch. Press seam toward the lining.

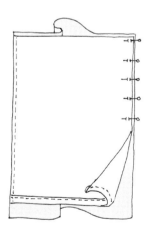

6. Turn panels right side out. Arrange the panel so that the fabric panel wraps around to the back, equal on each side. It should wrap evenly from the top of the curtain to the bottom hem. Press.

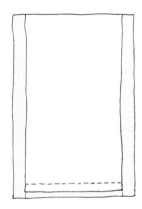

Lining Method with Mitered Corners

1. Follow Steps #1 and 2 for Basic Lining Method.

2. Hem lining using a 3" double hem.

3. Next, follow Steps #4 through 6 for Basic Lining Method.

4. To miter corners at bottom of panels, fold bottom edge up 4" to wrong side and press.

5. With wrong side facing you, diagonally fold under (at 45° angle) the bottom corner of each side hem until the point of each corner meets the inside edge of the side hem. Press in place.

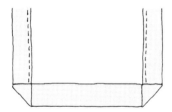

6. Fold bottom edge up 4" again and press. Hand stitch in place.

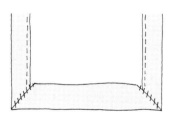

Basic Rod Pocket Curtains (page 72)

This is an easy window treatment, suitable for beginners. The pocket is actually a casing that slides over a rod or pole. A heading can also be created above the pocket to form a ruffle if desired.

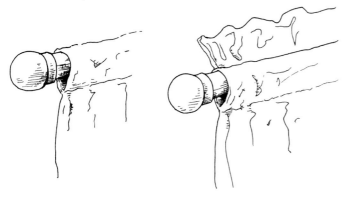

1. Refer to "Rod Sizes" chart for rod type to determine size of pocket.

2. Determine finished length for curtains and then add size of pocket, take-up allowance, desired heading size, $\frac{1}{2}$" turn under and 8" for a 4" double hem.

3. For fabric width, measure 2 $\frac{1}{2}$ times the length of the rod for fullness and add 4" for 1" double side hems. If needed add extra widths for your treatment. Cut the fabric according to your measurements.

4. Hem the side edges of curtains and press.

5. Hem the bottom of window treatment and press.

6. To make the pocket, fold $\frac{1}{2}$" of top edge to wrong side of fabric. Press.

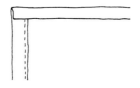

7. Add measurements for the pocket size, take-up and heading together. Using this measurement, again fold top edge of panel to wrong side of fabric. Press and stitch in place at lower edge.

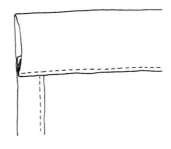

8. For heading, measure down from the top edge of panel for the desired size and mark across panel. Stitch along marking.

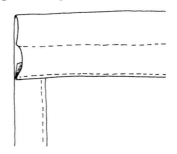

9. Slide panel onto rod.

Rod Sizes

Type of rod	Take-Up	Size of Pocket
3" pole	2"	5 $\frac{1}{2}$"
2 $\frac{1}{2}$" pole	1 $\frac{1}{2}$"	4"
2" pole	1 $\frac{1}{2}$"	4"
1-$\frac{3}{8}$" pole	1"	2 $\frac{1}{2}$"
$\frac{5}{8}$" pole	$\frac{1}{2}$"	1 $\frac{1}{2}$"
$\frac{3}{4}$" rod	$\frac{1}{4}$"	1 $\frac{1}{2}$"
$\frac{3}{8}$" rod	no take-up	1"

If interlining, or using thick fabric, add $\frac{1}{2}$" to pocket size.

If using lining, cut 4" shorter than curtain fabric.

If using interlining, cut it 8" shorter than curtain fabric.

Flat Curtains with Rings (example page 78)

1. When determining the finished width of drapes, use a 2 to 1 fullness ratio. Follow instructions 1 through 3 (Basic Flat Panels, page 99).

2. Sew a ring at each corner of panel, then space the others evenly across the top. For a no-sew option, use café clips.

Tab Top Curtains (example page 54)

These curtains have a crisp, casual look and are hung on café or pole rods.

1. Determine the width of curtain by measuring the rod, then double that figure for fullness. Add 4" for 1" double side hems.

2. To figure length of tabs, loop a measuring tape over the top part of the rod to desired length. Add 1" to this measurement for seam allowance. For width, double the desired width of tab and add $\frac{1}{2}$" for seam.

3. Hang rod. Since the finished length may vary with the tab length, measure from rod to floor (or 2 - 4" below window for shorter version) to determine length of panels. Add 8" for 4" double hem and $\frac{1}{2}$" for top seam. Add length of tab to this measurement (usually 2" - 2 $\frac{1}{2}$").

4. Cut a piece of fabric (facing) the width of the curtain by 6" long.

5. To figure how many tabs you need per panel, divide the width of the panel by the space desired between tabs (usually 5" to 6"). Add one to that number for the number of tabs needed. Mark position of tabs evenly spaced along top edge of panel.

6. You can make your tabs using one long strip. For example, cut the strip 2 $\frac{1}{2}$" wide by about 36". Fold the strip in half lengthwise with right sides together (A) and stitch along the raw edge with a $\frac{1}{4}$" seam allowance(B). Turn right side out and press with the seam toward the center(C). Cut the strip into 6" lengths.

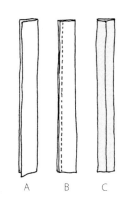

A   B   C

7. Fold tabs in half, matching the raw edges and center back seams with the center seam to the inside. Pin the tabs with raw edges to top of panel. The end tabs should be placed 2 $\frac{1}{4}$" in on each side to allow for 1" double side seams.

The center of the tab should fall at each mark you made previously.

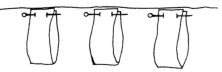

8. Prepare facing: Sew a hem by turning one edge under $\frac{1}{4}$" to the wrong side, press, then turn under $\frac{1}{2}$", pin and stitch. Line up the right sides of the facing and panel matching raw edges. Pin and stitch the facing to the top of curtain, with the tabs sandwiched in between.

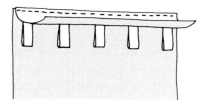

9. Open out the facing, press. Make a 1" double hem on each side of panel and facing. Turn the facing to the wrong side along the top seam line and press.

10. Topstitch each end of the facing to the hemmed edges of the panel.

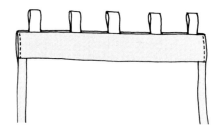

Hint: After pinning hem in place and before stitching, slide the panels on the rod to double check the length. If necessary, hem size can be adjusted at this point. Hem the bottom with a 4" double hem.

11. Slide the panel with tabs over the rod.

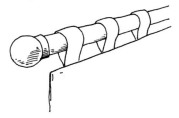

Cuffed Curtains (example page 30)

This type of window treatment looks great when using two coordinating fabrics. It's also a perfect treatment for a shower curtain.

1. To construct panels follow instructions #1 and 2 for Basic Flat Panels (page 99). In addition, for cuffed curtains you will need to add $1/2$" to the length for the seam allowance.

2. Cut cuff and lining fabric so that cut width is equal to the finished width of the panel. Cut length to desired size (usually 6"), plus $1/2$" on all sides for seam allowance.

3. Pin cuff and lining fabric right sides together. Stitch down one short end and across the width and up the other short end with $1/2$" seams. Clip the stitched corners diagonally. Turn right side out and press.

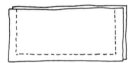 

4. Cut facing fabric so that it is equal to the width of the panel plus 1". Press under $1/2$" on each side and on bottom.

5. Pin the wrong side of the cuff to the right side of the panel.

6. Pin facing to upper edge of cuff, right sides together with all edges even. Stitch across top edge through all layers using $1/2$" seam allowance.

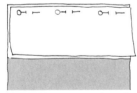

7. Fold facing up and over to back of panel, press.

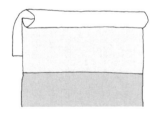

8. Stitch facing to back of panel along long ends and sides.

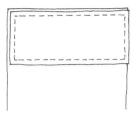

9. Rings should be spaced evenly, starting $1/2$" in from each edge and approximately 6" to 8" apart. Mark placement. Handstitch rings at each mark.

10. Slide rings onto the rod and arrange folds.

Banner Valance (example page 36)

Supplies needed:
Mounting board (1" x 4" cut to width of window)
Hardware to mount board to wall
Valance and lining fabric
Paper
Staple gun

1. Measure window to determine the size of the banner.

2. Make a pattern using a large sheet of paper. Hold the pattern up to the window to decide on size and length.

3. Pin pattern piece to fabric and lining fabric and cut out.

4. Place the fabric and lining right sides together and stitch the sides and bottom. Stitch down to the point and then up the other side.

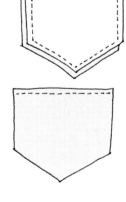

5. Turn right side out. Turn top edges under $1/2$" and stitch.

6. Drape top of banner 1" over top edge of mounting board and staple. Install the board on the wall.

Awning Valance (example page 54)

1. Mount a regular curtain rod to top of window, then a valance rod of desired length below the regular rod. (A valance rod has a longer projection.)

2. Measure the width of curtain rod and add measurement for two returns plus 4" for 1" double side hems.

3. Measure width of valance rod and add measurements for two returns plus 4" for side hems.

4. For length measurement, measure distance between the rods, plus amount needed for casing on top and bottom of valance and rod take up for both rods.

5. Cut fabric to width measurement for valance rod and to length measurement.

6. Find center of width and mark on top edge of fabric. Divide cutting measurement for curtain rod in half. Measure out from center on both sides and mark this measurement.

7. Draw a line from marks to bottom corners of valance. Cut along these lines.

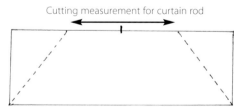

8. Sew side hems using 1" double hem. Construct rod pockets on top and bottom of valance using instructions on page 101. Thread rod through casings and hang.

Rolled Shade (example page 75)

Supplies needed:
Fabric - checked, floral and striped
Covered button kit
Spring pressure rod
Cardboard tube (the width of window)

1. Measure the inside of window frame for shade width. Determine the length desired.

2. Cut one piece each of the checked and the floral fabric to those measurements adding 1" for side seam allowances and 2 1/2" to length for casing and seams.

3. Place fabric pieces right sides together and sew around sides and bottom leaving top open.

4. Trim seams, turn right side out and press.

5. For casing, fold top edge 1" to back of panel, then fold 1" again and press. Stitch along bottom edge of fold to make casing.

6. Make two fabric bands using the striped fabric (see Ties and Bands page 111) twice the length of the fabric panel plus 3".

7. Make covered buttons using the floral fabric and sew evenly spaced along the bands (refer to photograph on page 75 for placement.)

8. Fold bands in half and slide over fabric panel at sides, placing fold at top and evenly spaced from each edge. Pin bands at top to hold and tack in place, align bands on back with bottom edge of shade and tack in place.

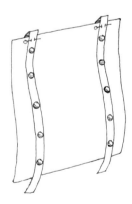

9. Thread shade onto the spring rod and place in window frame.

10. Place cardboard tube at bottom edge and roll panel to front to desired length. Pin the bands around the rolled fabric to back of shade and tack in place. If you'd like to be able to adjust the shade, add Velcro® dots to back of bands for closure.

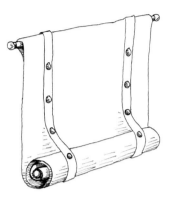

Optional: for a quick alternative, use wide ribbons instead of the fabric bands.

Bamboo Valance (example page 28)

Supplies needed:
Print and solid fabrics
Bamboo shade
Glue gun and glue sticks
Craft glue

1. Decide length of shade treatment and add 1" to measurement. Depending on the length of the valance desired, you may want to either roll it up or cut it. To cut shade, run a line of glue across width of shade at desired measurement and cut just below the glue line.

2. To make the fabric bands, cut print fabric double the size of desired width of the bands plus 1" for seam allowance. To calculate length of fabric, measure from top of bamboo valance to bottom edge and add 1" for seam allowance, 2" for turn-under at top and 1" for turn-under at bottom of shade.

3. Cut solid fabric following above instructions, adding 1" to width.

4. Fold printed fabric in half lengthwise with right sides together. Stitch $1/2$" on opposite side of fold and one short side.

5. Turn band right side out and press with the seam toward the center. Fold raw edges of open end under $1/2$" and sew closed. Press.

6. Repeat this same procedure for the solid fabric.

7. Position solid band on valance and glue in place at top and bottom using craft glue. Place print band over the top of solid band and glue to secure. Turn bottom of valance under 1" and glue. Turn the bands under and glue to back.

8. Mount the shade according to manufacturer's instructions.

Curtains with Binding Strips (page 60)

1. Measure and cut four contrasting strips for each curtain panel, two side strips and a strip for the top and bottom. Cut the top and bottom strips the width of the panel plus 1" for seam allowance. The side strips are cut to the length of the panel plus 1". All strips are cut four times the desired width. (Note: average width is from 2 - 3").

2. With wrong sides together, fold strips in half lengthwise and press.

3. Unfold strip. Fold each side to the center, the edges meeting at the crease. Press.

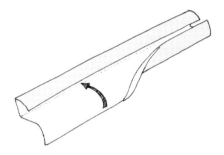

4. Open top strip along one edge and with right sides together, pin to panel matching top edges.

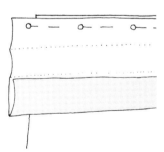

(Continued)

5. Clip excess fabric on end of strip to match panel.

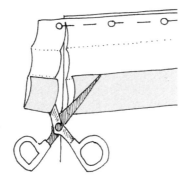

6. Stitch strip to panel along crease line.

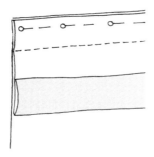

7. Encase the edge by folding the strip to the wrong side of the panel. Pin in place and stitch by hand.

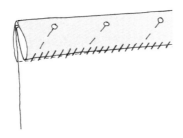

8. Stitch side strips to the panel in the same manner, but fold the ends to the inside instead of trimming them off.

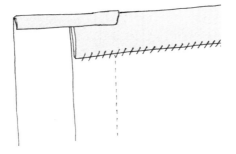

9. Encase the edge as shown and stitch by hand.

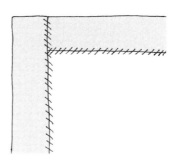

Flip-Over Valance

1. Measure the length of the rod between the brackets. This will be the measurement for the finished width of valance. Add 1" to measurement for seam allowance.

2. To determine the length of the valance, measure from the top of the rod to the area of the window where you want the valance to fall. Add 1" to measurement for seam allowance.

3. Cut two pieces of fabric to these measurements

4. Pin fabric with right sides together.

5. Stitch a $1/2$" seam around sides and bottom of valance leaving top open.

6. Turn valance right side out and hand stitch opening closed.

7. Flip valance over rod and panel and tack valance on each side.

Box Pleats

Box pleats are used on stationary treatments such as dust ruffles, valances, and chair slipcovers. To create pleats use Gosling® Folding Tape.

1. Cut fabric 2 $1/2$ times the finished width of the area to be pleated. Determine desired length adding fabric for 2" double hem, plus 1 $1/2$".

2. Machine baste the Gosling® tape along the raw edge on the wrong side of fabric. Pull cords forming the pleats.

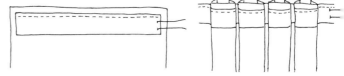

3. Press in the pleats. Just below the folding tape, machine baste to hold pleats in place.

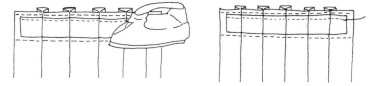

4. Remove the tape by pulling out the basting stitches. Trim 1" from the raw edge.

5. Box pleats are now ready to attach to treatment.

Flip-Over Valance with Box Pleats
(example page 63)

1. Follow Steps #1 through 5 for Flip Over Valance.

2. Then, follow Steps #1 through 4 for Box Pleats.

3. Place right sides of valance and box pleats together matching raw edges at top. Pin in place and stitch using $1/_2$" seam allowance.

4. Trim seam $1/_4$" and press seam down toward valance on wrong side.

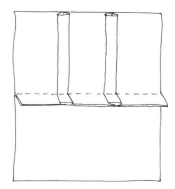

5. Turn valance over and with valance and pleats laying flat, top stitch along seam line.

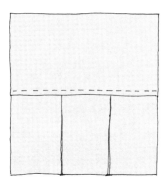

6. Flip over rod on top of curtain panel. Tack at sides to secure, if desired.

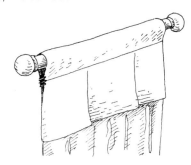

Balloon Valance (example page 57)

Supplies needed:
Decorator fabric
Fabric for lining
Shirring tape or fusible shirring tape

1. For the width of the valance, cut the fabric two times the measurement of the window plus 1" for $1/_2$" seams.

2. Decide the finished length for the valance. Allow extra fabric for a rod casing plus $1/_2$" for bottom hem.

3. Cut the lining fabric to the above measurements.

4. Cut enough pieces of shirring tape to space evenly across width of shade. Allow from 15" to 20" between each piece. The length of each piece should be $1/_3$ of the finished valance.

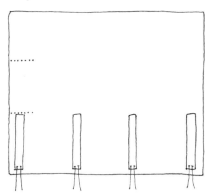

5. Place right sides of fabric and lining together. Stitch $1/_2$" seams on sides and bottom. Turn right side out and press.

6. Make rod casing at top of valance (see page 101).

(Continued)

7. Position shirring tape on bottom edge of valance and fuse in place.

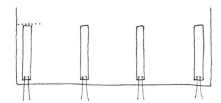

8. To gather, pull the cords and tie together to secure.

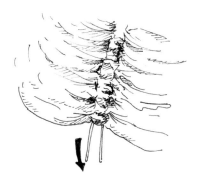

9. Slide valance on rod.

Cafe Curtains (example page 44)

Supplies needed:
Fabric
Plastic rings
Tension rods
Foam core
Craft knife
Hot glue gun and glue sticks

1. For curtains pictured on page 44, make two basic panels (see Basic Flat Panel Instructions page 99). Hang with small white rings on a tension rod.

2. Make the valance using two strips of contrasting fabric. The length of one strip is cut larger than the other.

3. After sewing the side seams and hem on each fabric strip, pin right side of the smaller strip to

wrong side of the wider strip at top and stitch together.

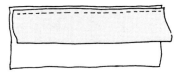

4. Flip the small strip to front of wider strip and press. Space the small white rings evenly across the top and hand sew in place.

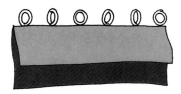

5. Slip the rings onto the rod.

6. Use the tea cup pattern on page 127 to trace the design onto foam core. Cut out the desired number of tea cup shapes using a craft knife.

7. Use the foam core shapes to trace around on back of fabric. Add 1" all around and cut out.

8. Clip fabric all around about $1/4$" from traced shape. Inside of handle: cut an X (as shown) with a craft knife or sharp small scissors.

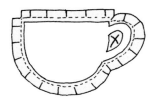

9. Spread a thin layer of white craft glue on foam core cup. Place this on top of back side of fabric.

10. Spread glue around edge of back of cup and fold fabric pieces up and into glue. Use glue on fingertips to neaten corners. Cover back with fabric, if desired.

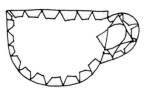

11. When glue is dry, hot glue the cups to the rod.

Pleated Drapes (example page 16)

Pleater tapes help to form even pleats on draperies. There are several types of pleater tapes available. Follow manufacturer's instructions for each tape.

1. Make basic panels (see instructions page 99).

2. At the top of the drape, turn under 2" toward wrong side of fabric, press(A). Pin tape to wrong side of drape and fold ends of tape under(B).

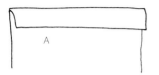 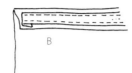

Pin cords out of the way. Stitch across top and bottom of tape.

3. Tie off one end of drawstrings. Pull the free end of string to pleat. Tie the drawstrings into bows.

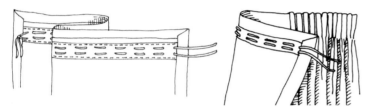

4. Sew on rings to top edge of panel or use clip-on rings. Place on rod.

If using pleater tape with pockets, follow instructions above, then insert pronged ends of drapery hooks into pockets on tape to form the pleats. Hang drapes on traverse rods.

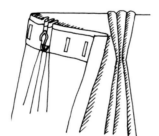

Setting the pleats

1. Hand press the pleats in the drapes. Then wrap the drapes with strips of fabric and pin them.

2. Use an iron to steam the drapes and let them set for two or three days. Remove the strips.

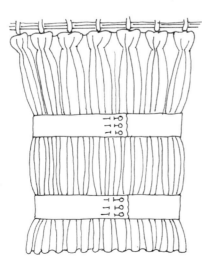

Roman Shade (example page 55)

This window treatment is informal and casual. It's slightly tedious to construct but well worth the trouble when completed.

Supplies needed:
Fabric
Mounting board (1" x 4")
Roman shade tape
Nylon cord
Screw eyes
Awning cleat
Weighted pull
Velcro® strip
1 $\frac{1}{2}$" x $\frac{1}{4}$" lattice strip

1. Determine the amount of tape to purchase by multiplying the width of shade by the number of rows you'll want on your shade.

2. Rows of tape should be spaced 8" - 12" apart and you'll need a row for each side of shade.

3. For shades inside window casing, measure inside frame minus $\frac{1}{2}$" for finished width. Install using angle irons.

4. For shades to be hung outside of window, measure from frame plus 1" for finished width. Mount board above window.

5. For length, measure from top of mounting board to window sill.

6. Cut fabric finished width plus 5", finished length plus 9".

7. Place fabric wrong side up and press double hems 1 $\frac{1}{4}$" on sides, 2 $\frac{1}{2}$" on bottom, and 2" on top edge. Pin all hems in place.

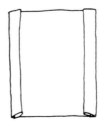 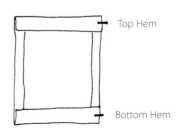

Top Hem

Bottom Hem

(Continued)

8. Pin ring tape over the side hems and evenly spaced across shade. Bottom rings should be 3" above the top of lower hem.

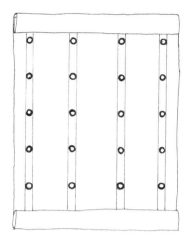

9. The tape should extend 1" under the top and bottom hem. Stitch each strip of tape along both long edges (folding the top and bottom hems out of the way). Refold bottom hem and stitch.

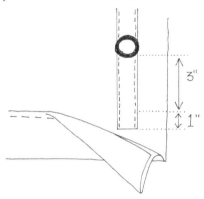

10. Fold open top hem to first fold. Sew Velcro® strip $1/4$" from fold line. Sew along both sides of strip. Refold hem and stitch along bottom fold.

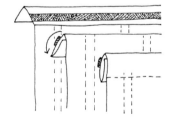

11. Insert the lattice strip in bottom hem (pocket).

12. Staple the hook side strip of Velcro® to the upper edge of mounting board front. Then attach shade to board with Velcro®.

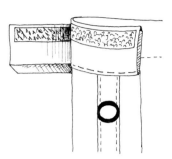

13. Line up the rings on the back of shade to board and mark with a pencil. Attach screw eyes to board at each mark.

14. Now you're ready to thread the cord through the rings. Tie a cord to each bottom ring of ring tape. Thread the cords up through the rings in that row. Next thread cords through the screw eye at the top of each row. Thread all cords going one way through each screw eye to one side of shade.

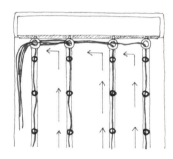

15. Mount the board at the window then adjust the cords so tension is equal. Tie cords in knot at corner. Then trim cords as shown leaving one cord as a pull. (add a weighted pull to the one cord).

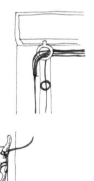

16 Attach cleat to wall or inside window frame.

17. Pull the shade up, adjusting the folds to hold shade in place, tie cord around cleat.

Ties and Bands

Bands can be used for stagecoach shades, for decorating matchstick shades, etc. Ties are used to tie back drapes and curtains, for seat cushions and for hanging draperies or curtains.

1. For fabric bands, determine length for your desired project and add 1" for seam allowance. The width of fabric should be double the desired size plus 1" for seam allowance. Cut fabric to those measurements.

2. Fold fabric in half lengthwise with right sides together(A). Stitch $1/2$" seam on opposite side of fold and one short side(B). Turn band right side out and press it so the seam falls at the center back of band(C).

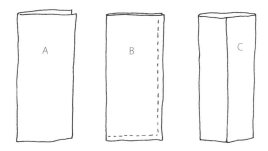

3. Fold raw edges of open end under $1/2$" (D) and sew closed (E).

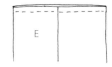

Both ties and bands can be embellished with trims and tassels.

> Hint: When cutting Styrofoam®, coat knife lightly with candle wax. For smooth edges, rub another piece of Styrofoam® along any rough edges.

Cornices

Making and Covering a Styrofoam® Cornice (example page 88)

For a formal, finished look or to hide unsightly hardware, a cornice is just the trick. Make it the easy way using Styrofoam® sheets and glue.

Supplies needed:
Styrofoam® sheets, 12" x 36"
Glue gun and low melt glue sticks
Quiliting pins or corrugated nails
Knife with serrated edge
Fabric
Batting (optional)

1. Measure width of window to determine length to cut Styrofoam®. Measure from outside edge of molding. Add 4" for length of Styrofoam® needed.

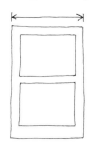

2. You will need 1 face board, 2 end pieces and a dust board

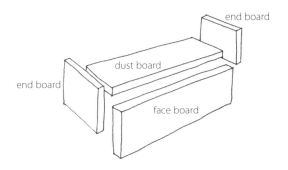

3. To make a design on the cornice (such as scallops), draw the design on paper for a pattern, then transfer the design to the Styrofoam®. Cut along your traced line, using a serrated knife.

(Continued)

4. If window is too long to use one sheet of Styrofoam®—place two sheets together and affix them using glue gun and low melt glue or use corrugated nails. Allow to dry thoroughly.

5. Glue end boards. Let the pieces dry overnight.

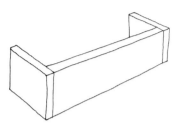

6. Glue dust board between the two end boards, 2" down from top. To cover the cornice , cut batting 1" wider than the face board and $1/_2$" less on each end. For a less "puffy" look, eliminate the batting.

7. Cut the fabric 9" longer and wider than the batting. You may have to piece the fabric. Be sure to match any patterns.

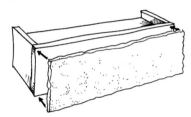

8. You can either seal the raw edges with white glue or run them through your serger.

9. Place batting at the top of the cornice and $1/_2$" in on each side. Pin or glue batting in place. Roll extra batting to the inside at top of cornice.

10. Place the cornice face down on the wrong side of the fabric. Allow equal amounts of fabric on each side and enough fabric on top to reach dust board edge.

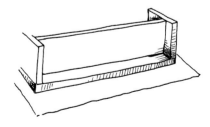

11. Wrap the fabric over the end boards toward the inside of cornice. Pin in place. Next, wrap the top and bottom fabric over the cornice to the inside.

Also pin in place.

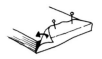

Note: when pinning fabric to cornice, start at center and work to each end. Place pins at a 45° angle in the opposite direction that you are pulling fabric. Be sure to check that fabric is taut and in alignment.

12. Trims may be applied after cornice is covered using either pins or glue.

Installing a Styrofoam® Cornice

Supplies needed:
Fabric covered cornice
Pencil
Angle brackets
Screws or toggle bolts
Level (optional)

Place the cornice board in the desired place over the window and center it. Mark with a pencil where the brackets will go. If desired, use a level to be sure the cornice board is perfectly level.

Attach the brackets to the wall with screws or toggle bolts. Then, place the cornice on the angle brackets and secure with screws.

Making a Wooden Cornice

Heavy wooden cornices are more difficult to construct than Styrofoam® ones. They're also more difficult to install. Wooden cornices are used primarily when the drapes are extremely heavy. If you wish to make one of wood, follow the instructions below.

Supplies needed:
1" x 4" board (cut to desired length)
Nails or wood glue

To figure the length needed, measure your window and add 2".

Nail or glue the pieces of wood together—the two end pieces to the face board and then the dust board at the top.

Installing a Wooden Cornice

This type of cornice should be used when hanging heavier window treatments

Supplies needed:
Cornice made from board (instructions page 112)
Angle brackets
Pencil
Screws or toggle bolts
Level (optional)

1. Prior to covering the cornice with fabric, measure and mark with a pencil where angle brackets should go on the bottom of the board. They should be an equal distance apart (allow 1" of space beyond each side edge of window frame).

2. Place cornice board over the window, centered, and mark the bracket placements on wall. A level is helpful to make sure board is straight.

3. Attach brackets to the wall where you had previously marked and screw them to the wall using screws or toggle bolts.

4. Now is the time to paint the board or cover with fabric (see instructions, page 112)

5. Place the painted or covered board on the brackets and attach the board to brackets.

Bar Stool Seat Covers (example page 43)

These are seats that are fabric-covered wood bases that fit onto a stool frame. Recovering these to match other fabrics in the room is easy. All you need is some fabric and an electric stapler.

1. Remove seat cushion. Measure the base and add 8". Make a paper pattern if desired. Place pattern on fabric and cut out. Cut a piece of batting the same size as the round wooden base.

2. Sew two rows of basting stitches 1" from the cut edge of fabric.

3. Center the base, face down on the circle of batting and the wrong side of the fabric.

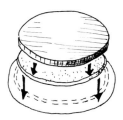

4. Draw up the gathers, secure the thread, then tack and staple the cover to the seat.

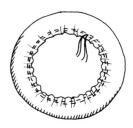

5. Glue or nail the covered seat onto the stool.

Covering a Chair Seat

You will need:

Fabric

Batting

Staple gun

1. Remove seat from chair. Draw around seat on wrong side of fabric. Cut out fabric 4" outside drawn line.

2. Cut batting same size as fabric. Layer batting, then fabric on seat. Fold fabric at corners diagonally over batting to fit seat corners. Alternating sides and pulling taut, staple edges of fabric to bottom of seat. Trim as necessary.

3. Reattach seat to chair.

Bedding

Refer to the diagram below when measuring for the bed covering you will be making.

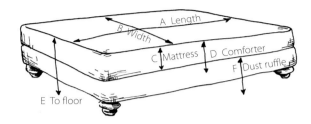

Basic Bedspread

1. Determine the size of the bedspread. For width, measure bed (see diagram above) B + 2 E's, add 4" for hem allowances.

2. For length, A + E + 30" for pillow-fold-over + 4" for hem allowance.

3. Since fabric doesn't come wide enough to make the bedspread, you will need to add side panels (never seam down the center). To figure the cut sizes of the three lengths of fabric: Use the width of the fabric, minus 1"(for seam allowances) for the center section. Subtract the center section from the finished width of the covering.

4. To figure how much fabric you'll need, multiply the length of the bedspread by the number of panels.

5. Cut the center panel and then another the same size. Cut the second panel down the center (these will be the two side panels).

6. Pin the side panels to the center panel right sides together, matching pattern in fabric if necessary. Sew side panels to center panel. Press seams open.

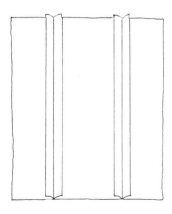

7. Hem the sides, then the top and bottom edges using a 1" double hem.

8. For a bedspread with rounded corners, fold the spread in half lengthwise, right sides together. Mark as in diagram below.

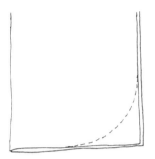

9. Trim along the marked line. Then finish bedspread referring to step #7.

Basic Comforter

1. Determine measurements and amount of fabric needed by following instructions for Basic Duvet on page 118. Subtract 1" from the length measurement. (comforter length = A + 12" + 1").

2. Cut top and bottom fabric to these measurements. Sew center panel and side panels together with $1/2$" seams.

3. With right sides together, pin top and bottom of comforter along sides and bottom. Sew using $1/2$" seam allowance.

4. Turn right side out and insert down comforter or synthetic filling.

5. Turn top edge under $1/2$" to wrong side of fabric. Press and hand sew the opening closed.

Dust Ruffles (example page 35)

The skirt of the dust ruffle is sewn to a piece of fabric called the deck (can be muslin, chintz or sheeting fabric).

Fabric needed for deck if using 54" wide fabric:

For a twin bed - 2 $1/8$ yd

For a full bed - 3 $1/8$ yd.

Queen - 3 $1/2$ yds.

King - 4 $1/2$ yds.

1. Measure for a dust ruffle by measuring A and B, then F to floor.

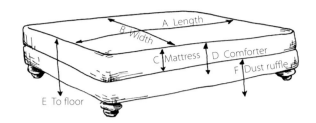

2. To make the deck, cut the deck fabric by adding 1" to B and 1" to A, then piece the fabric (see Basic Bedspread Instructions, page 114).

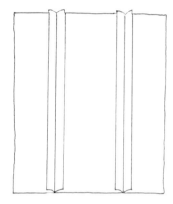

3. At top edge make a 1" double hem.

4. Mark the corners, then divide the deck into six-teenths and mark as below:

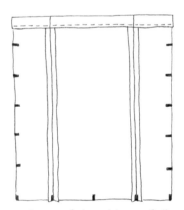

5. Figure dimensions of the skirt as follows:

Skirt depth - F + 2 $\frac{1}{2}$"

Sides - A x 2 $\frac{1}{2}$ (for fullness). Cut 2

End - B x 2 $\frac{1}{2}$ (for fullness). Cut 1

6. Cut and piece each side skirt, using $\frac{1}{2}$" seams.

7. Hem sides and bottom edge of each skirt using 1" double hems.

8. Machine gather the upper edge of skirts. Stitch first row of gathering stitches $\frac{1}{4}$" down from raw edge. Stitch second row $\frac{1}{4}$" down from first row.

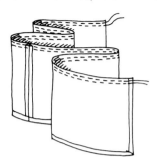

9. Divide each skirt into fourths and mark.

10. Gather skirts by gently pulling bobbin threads, securing threads at one end.

11. Pin one side skirt to one side edge of deck with right sides together, matching quarter marks. Adjust gathers to fit evenly between marks, and then stitch skirt to deck with $\frac{1}{2}$" seam. Then do the same for the other two skirts.

12. Press seams toward deck, then turn over and topstitch through all the layers.

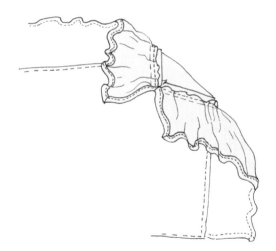

Dust Ruffle with Pleated Corners

(page 36)

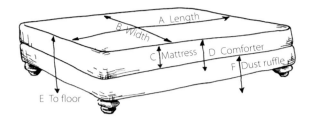

1. Cut and assemble the deck following Dust Ruffle instructions, steps 1 and 2, page 115.

2. To determine the cutting measurements for the skirt, add F + 2 $\frac{1}{2}$" for the depth and B + 2 x A + 80" for pleats, side hems and corner wrap-around for the length. Cut fabric to those measurements.

3. If you have to piece your fabric, try to center the seams on the skirt or pleat fold.

4. Hem the sides and bottom edge of ruffle using a 1" double hem.

5. To find the center, fold the skirt lengthwise with wrong sides together and mark at raw edges.

6. To mark for the four pleated corners, follow diagram.

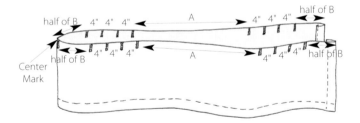

7. With right side up, fold and match marks to create pleat. Pin and press.

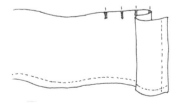

8. Staystitch across upper edge of pleat. Clip center of each pleat as shown.

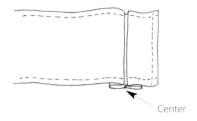

9. To attach skirt to deck, first fold deck in half lengthwise and mark center.

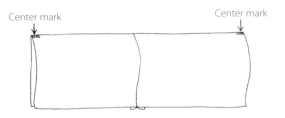

10. Pin the skirt to the deck matching center clip, darts to the corners of the deck. With right sides together, have skirt side facing up and stitch a $\frac{1}{2}$" seam pivoting at corners.

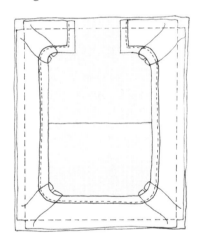

11. Finish by pressing the seam allowances toward the deck, and pressing upper edge under $\frac{1}{2}$" and stitch around the deck, stitching through all layers.

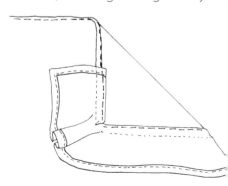

Flounced Bedspread (example page 32)

A flounced bedspread has a fitted top and gathered sides. You'll need to decide if you want the top of the bed covering to be of one fabric and the flounce of another.

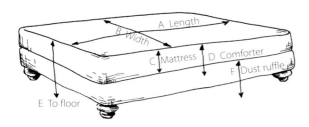

1. Figure the cutting measurements for the top of the bed covering:

    Top width - B + 1"

    Top length - A + 30" + 2 $\frac{1}{2}$" (allows for pillow foldover)

2. Figure cutting measurements for the flounce:

    Flounce depth - E + 2 $\frac{1}{2}$"

    Flounce length - B + 2 A's x 2 $\frac{1}{2}$ (for fullness)

3. Figure how much fabric you'll need (see page 114 Basic Bedspread, Step 3).

4. Figure the amount of fabric for flounce by multiplying the number of panels by the flounce depth.

5. Figure the sizes of the center and side panels (see page 114, Step 4).

6. Construct the top part of the bedspread by cutting and piecing as in Steps #4 through 6 of Basic Bedspread (page 114). Hem the upper edge with a 1" double hem.

7. Divide and mark the sides and lower edge of top into sixteenths as pictured in diagram.

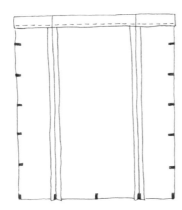

8. Cut and piece the flounce using $\frac{1}{2}$" seams.

9. Hem the sides and bottom edge of the flounce with 1" double hems.

10. Mark the upper edge of flounce into sixteenths.

11. Machine-gather the upper edge of flounce. Stitch first row of gathering stitches $\frac{1}{4}$" down from raw edge. Stitch second row $\frac{1}{4}$" down from first row. Gather flounce by gently pulling bobbin threads, securing threads at one end.

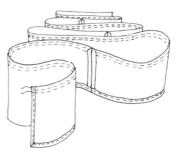

12. With right sides together, pin the flounce to the top, matching the markings you made previously. Adjust gathers, then stitch flounce to top with a $\frac{1}{2}$" seam.

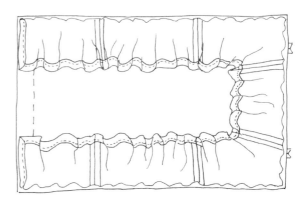

Double Flounce Bedspread (page 32)

Cut a second flounce, two-thirds the depth of the first flounce. Piece and hem the two flounces separately. Baste them together along the top edge. Gather and attach as one unit to the top, following Step #12 above.

Basic Duvet (example page 31)

A Duvet is just like a big pillowcase. It's not sewn closed, so the comforter inside can be removed and the duvet laundered. It should be made from a lightweight, easy-to-launder fabric, one that coordinates nicely with the dust ruffle and pillow shams.

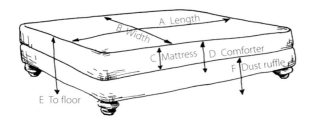

1. To determine cutting dimensions for top and bottom piece of duvet:

Length - A + 12" for drop at end of bed + 2" for hem and seam

Width - B + 12" x 2 for side drops + 2" seam allowance

2. Since fabric doesn't come wide enough to make the duvet, you will need to add side panels. Never seam down the center. To determine size of panels, measure the width of fabric minus 1" for seam allowances and subtract from finished width of the duvet. Divide the difference equally and cut the fabric into side panels to this measurement.

3. To determine the amount of fabric you will need, multiply the measurement for the length times the number of panels you will need. You will need the same amount for the bottom of duvet cover.

4. Pin the side panels to the center panel with right sides together. Match pattern in fabric if necessary. Stitch together with $1/2$" seams. Repeat this for bottom panels.

5. With right sides together, pin top and bottom of duvet together. Stitch bottom and sides together with $1/2$" seams.

6. Turn top edge under $1/2$" to wrong side and press. Turn under again 1" to wrong side and hem by hand or machine.

7. Velcro® strips may be used for closure.

Fitted Bedspread (example page 35)

1. For fabric measurements determine the width, B + 2 C's, for length A + 2 C's. Add 8" for a 1" double hem on all four sides.

2. Cut fabric to these measurements (a quilted fabric is an ideal choice for this type of bedspread).

3. Follow steps #3 through 6 for Basic Bedspread (page 114).

4. Turn bottom edge of all four sides under $1/2$" and press. Turn edges under again 1" and pin in place.

5. Machine stitch along edge to form casing leaving a 1" opening for $3/4$" elastic.

6. Thread elastic through casing. Machine stitch ends of elastic together and stitch opening of casing closed.

Fitted Bedspread with Darts (page 36)

1. For fabric measurements see Step #1 of Fitted Bedspread, above).

2. Then follow Steps #3 through 6 for Basic Bedspread (page 114).

3. Place bedspread on bed, wrong side up. Make sure drops are even all the way around. Mark one

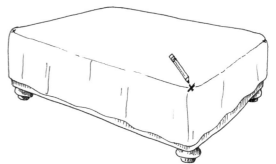

corner where the dart is to end on top edge of bedspread.

4. Measure from edge of corner to mark and then mark the remaining corners, according to your measurements.

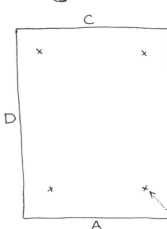

5. With right sides together, fold side A to meet side B matching edges. Stitch from mark, straight down to edge of spread.

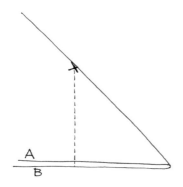

6. Repeat in each corner, B to C, C to D, D to A. See diagram page 118.

7. Clip darts and press open.

8. Finish with a 1" double hem around the bed spread.

Place Mats (example page 45)

The standard size of a place mat is 12" x 18".

1. For one place mat, cut two pieces of fabric 12" x 18" plus $1/2$" all around for hems.

2. Cut a piece of batting 11 $1/2$" x 17 $1/2$".

3. Place fabric right sides together, pin, then stitch three sides. Turn fabric right side out.

4. Slide batting piece inside place mat. Turn raw edges of opening under $1/2$" and pin in place.

5. Topstitch around all four sides $1/4$" in from edge, then topstitch again around all four sides $1/4$" in from first topstitch.

Napkins (example page 45)

The standard size of a napkin is 18" x 20"

1. Cut fabric 19" x 21".

2. Hem the napkin using a $1/4$" double hem.

Fresh Start

The following instructions are for the projects created for the condominium in the "Fresh Start" Chapter (see photos pages 69 - 89).

Master Bedroom

Duvet with Accent Panel (Page 83)

1. Construct the duvet as in Basic Duvet, page 118.

2. Cut fabric for accent piece (contrasting fabric that is sewn to lower end of duvet top.) Fabric should be the same width as the duvet plus 1" for seam allowances. For the length, cut fabric 20".

3. Turn top edge of accent fabric under 1 $1/2$" to wrong side and hem in place using iron-on hemming tape.

4. Lay accent fabric on lower end of top piece of duvet matching bottom edges and side edges. Both duvet top and accent fabric should be facing up.

5. Using $1/2$" seams, baste accent piece to duvet cover along side and lower edges.

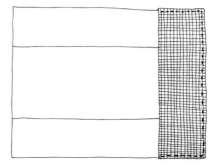

6. Lay bottom of duvet on duvet top with right sides together. Pin in place and stitch around sides and lower edge with $1/2$" seam. Turn right side out.

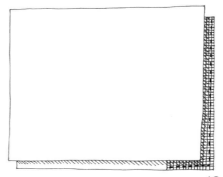

(Continued)

7. Turn top edge under $1/2$" to wrong side and press. Turn under again 1" to wrong side and hem by hand or machine.

8. Use Velcro® strips for closure.

9. Cover six large buttons with fabric and sew on accent fabric as pictured.

Drapes

1. Hang single curtain rods 1" from ceiling along window wall and portions of alcove side walls.

2. Measure for draperies from rod to floor.

3. Make four rod pocket drapery panels (see instructions page 101) for the window treatment.

Fabric Shade with Banner Valance

1. Use spring pressure rods for this treatment.

2. Hang the rods on the inside top and bottom casing of the window. Cut fabric to window measurement allowing enough for top and bottom rod pockets.

3. For banner, make a paper pattern according to window size, then follow instructions for making a banner valance on page 103. Sew a tassel to the point of the banner.

Swagged Table Topper (example page 83)

This topper uses two-cord shirring tape.

1. For the amount of shirring tape required, multiply the drop measurement of the table by 6 and add 12"

2. Make the round cloth (see page 92).

3. On the wrong side, divide and mark the edge of the topper into six equal parts. Mark the center.

4. Cut the shirring tape into six pieces (the drop measurement plus 2".) Use a pin to pull out 1 $1/2$" of the draw cords at each end. Trim off 1" of tape only and press the tape under $1/2$".

5. Pin the tape to the wrong side of the topper at markings so that one end is $1/2$" above the hem and tape points toward the center of the topper.

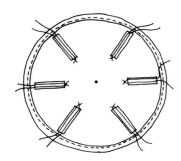

6. Stitch on both edges of tape, backstitching at the beginning and end.

7. Tie each cord end nearest the center into a knot and secure with glue.

8. Center the topper on the table. (Place something heavy on the table to secure topper). Pull on one of the sets of cords adjusting the swag to the desired depth. Tie the cord ends in a bow. Do the same with the other cords until all match.

Small Bedroom

Large Window

1. Instructions for constructing and covering a cornice are on page 111. Glue white rope cording around edges of cornice for trim.

2. Rod pocket curtains were hung under cornice and tied back with the same white rope cording.

Small Window

Decorated roll-up shade was constructed from a kit Complete instructions are included in each kit. The same (but smaller) cornice as on large window was constructed for this window. As a variation to the kit, decorative cording was added to this shade.

Starry Night Lampshade (page 90)

Self adhesive lampshade
Fabric
White rope cord
Glue gun and glue sticks
Fabric glue

1. The self adhesive shade includes a cutting pattern. Lay the pattern on the wrong side of the fabric and trace.

2. Cut fabric and then hand-press it to the sticky shade.

3. Spread fabric glue along the overlapping edge of the fabric and press down to secure.

4. Measure the top and bottom diameters of the lampshade and cut rope cord to that measurement adding 1".

5. Hot glue the cord to the top and bottom edge of shade, trim cord, butt up ends and glue to secure.

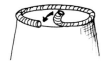

Hint: When using braids or cords that unravel easily, place a small piece of tape around the cord and then cut through it in the center so that both ends are taped (like a shoelace). Work with the cord taped, then remove it after it is affixed and secured to your project, either by gluing or sewing.

Kitchen

Tab Top Café Curtains and Valance

1. Window treatment was hung inside casing. Spring pressure rods were used.

2. Top treatment is a rod pocket valance with ruffle (instructions page 101).

3. Tab top curtains (page 102) were made using grosgrain ribbon spaced evenly across the top.

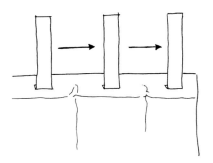

4. Ribbon tabs were affixed to panel using iron-on hemming tape (with ends of ribbon turned under $\frac{1}{4}$"). Buttons were sewn on for decoration and added strength.

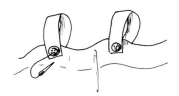

Living Room

Drapes

Rod pocket panels (see instructions page 101) were hung on either side of the window on a white wooden rod with ball finials. A rod pocket valance with ruffle (see instructions page 101) was hung between the two panels.

Pillows

A collection of knife edge pillows (instructions page 94) in blue and white plaids decorate the white wicker chair along with a comfy seat cushion (instructions page 124).

Rolled Shade

See page 104 for instructions.

Dining Room

Flat Panel Drapes with Rings

1. Flat panel drapes with rings (see instructions page 99) were hung on white wooden rod with ball finials.

Swags

Swags are top treatments for windows. They can stand alone or be combined with curtains, drapes, cascades or other embellishments such as jabots and rosettes.

The swag can be gently draped on a pole, attached to a board or placed in swag holders.

The fabric for a swag should be soft so that it drapes nicely.

Swags should be installed 8" above the window or at the ceiling.

Basic Swag

1. Measure the distance between the swag holders (A), then measure down from the holders to the desired length of tails (B&C). Add these measurements together + 1" for seam allowance to determine the total cutting length. The cutting width depends on how wide or narrow you want the swag to be.

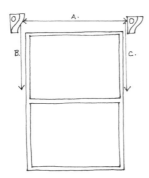

2. Cut a rectangle of fabric to those measurements.

3. Measure in 18" (depending on the size of the cascade angle desired) at each lower corner, then draw a diagonal line from the upper corner to the mark

at bottom edge and cut along the marked line. Do the same with the lining fabric.

4. Place the two pieces of fabric right sides together and sew, leaving an opening for turning. Turn right side out and hand sew the opening closed.

5. Press the swag, then fold into pleats and drape over the holders.

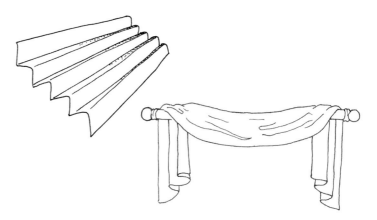

Rod Pocket Drapes with Swag

The rod pocket drapes (see page 101) were hung on a white wooden rod.

A swag of two coordinating fabrics was draped over the window treatment on the same rod.

Use medium weight fabrics so that swag will drape nicely.

1. Cut fabric to appropriate measurement (See Basic Swag Instructions, Step 1). Place the two fabrics right sides together. Sew along three edges with $1/2$" seam allowance. Sew fourth edge leaving a 3" opening to turn. Press seams open. Turn right side out and hand sew opening closed.

2. Fan fold fabric lengthwise into about 3 folds.

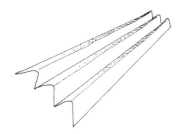

3. Drape over pole arranging folds as desired. Adjust side cascades.

(Hint – if you get tired of your swag, reverse it so the other fabric will show for a pleasant change.)

Chandelier Shades (page 78)

Supplies needed:
6 small self adhesive lampshades
Fabric
Gimp trim
Fabric glue

1. Follow same instructions for Starry Night Lampshade (page 121).

2. After applying fabric, cut, then glue gimp trim around top and bottom edge of each shade. Trim, then butt edges of trim together and glue to secure.

Chair Cushions (example page 78)

Supplies needed:
Fabric
Polyester fiberfill
Upholstery needle
Covered button kit
Large paper for pattern

1. Cut a piece of fabric twice as long as A + 5". For width, B + 4".

2. Place paper on chair and trace around it for a pattern.

3. Fold fabric in half. Place front part of pattern 1" in from fold of fabric. Mark pattern on fabric adding 1 $\frac{1}{2}$" on sides and back. Cut along markings.

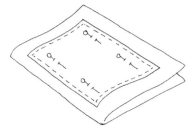

4. Follow instructions on page 111 to make fabric ties. You will need two 20" ties per cushion.

(Continued)

5. Fold ties in half and position on back of cushion with fold of tie aligned with raw edge of cushion.

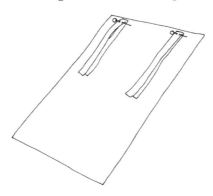

6. Fold fabric in half right sides together, sandwiching ties in between. Stitch sides and back of cushion with $1/2$" seam allowance leaving an opening in back for stuffing.

7. To make a box edge on each corner of cushion, open out seams to lay flat. Pin, then stitch across $1/2$" from ends and trim.

Repeat Steps 7 for each corner of cushion.

8. Trim corners and turn cushion right side out.

9. Fill with polyester fiberfill and hand stitch opening closed.

10. Cover buttons following manufacturer's instructions on package.

11. Mark desired position of buttons on both front and back of cushion. Make sure marks align.

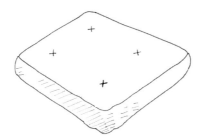

12. Cut thread long enough to go through cushion and for tying buttons on both sides.

13. Draw needle and thread from back to front of cushion and thread on button (do not pull thread all the way through). Using a slip knot, attach button loosely.

14. Repeat on back side of cushion. After all buttons are in place, secure tightly by pulling slip knot.

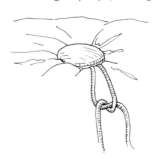

Calculating Yardage for Window Treatments

	Sample	*Your figures*

1. Widths of fabric needed

Rod length	.72"	_____
Multiply for fullness (2 $\frac{1}{2}$", 3", 3 $\frac{1}{2}$")	x 2.5	_____
	= 180"	_____
Add overlap and return (12" for single rod, 16" for double rod)	+ 12"	_____
Width of fabric	=192"	_____
Divided by fabric width	÷ 54"	_____
	= 3.5	_____
Round up to next whole number	= 4	_____

2. Length

Finished length	.80"	_____
Hems and headings (usually 4 double hems and headings)	+16"	_____
Equals cut length (for solid fabrics only)	= 96"	_____
Divide by a pattern repeat	÷ 25"	_____
Equals number of repeats per length	= 3.84	_____
Round up to next whole number	= 4	_____
Multiply repeats needed by length of repeat	25" x 4	_____
Equals adjusted cut length	100"	_____

3. Total yardage

Multiply number of widths by the adjusted cut length (#1 x #2)	100" x 4 = 400"	_____
Divide by 36"	÷ 36"	
Equals Total Yardage needed (per treatment)	= 12 yds.	_____

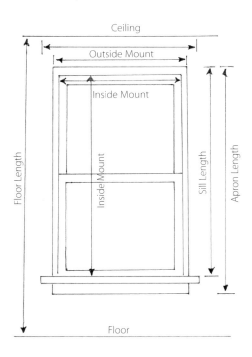

Glossary

Bias: 45° diagonal direction between lengthwise and crosswise threads of fabric.

Bullion fringe: Long silky fringe used to trim cushions and drapes.

Café curtain: A short curtain hung with a rod.

Casing: A pocket made to hold a curtain rod. Usually a double hem at top of curtain or drape.

Cleat: A metal or plastic device attached to side of window to hold cords for adjustable window treatments.

Cornice: A horizontal decorative box used to hide a curtain rod, usually covered with fabric.

Curtain: A decorative window covering, usually unlined.

Curtain drop: The finished length of curtain or drop from the rod to bottom edge.

Cut length: The finished length of curtain or drapes, plus allowances for headers, hems, and take-up.

Cut width: The finished width plus allowances for side hems and seams.

Decorator fabric: The main or outer fabric, used for the treatment. Also known as "face fabric".

Double hem: A hem where the fabric is turned under twice.

Drapery: Decorative window covering, usually lined and extending to the floor.

Drop length: The distance from the top of the treatment to where the fabric ends.

Fabric panel: Term to describe treatment when all the widths of fabric are sewn together (often one width of fabric is enough for panel).

Facing: A piece of fabric used to add more strength to main fabric.

Finial: Decorative end of curtain rod.

Finished length: The length of curtain or drape after header and hem are sewn.

Finished width: The width of fabric after seams and side hems are sewn.

Gather: Method to pull fabric tighter to add fullness.

Header: Fabric above rod pocket usually for decorative purpose.

Heading: The area at the top of curtain or drape, which includes tape, ties, rings, rod pocket, ruffle, etc.

Interlining: Additional fabric sewn between decorator fabric and lining to help keep light out and to provide additional insulation.

Lining: Fabric sewn on back of main fabric to help protect from light and give a neat finish.

Miter: A sewing technique to join pieces of fabric with a diagonal seam to form a flat corner.

Mounting board: A piece of wood usually 1" x 4" to which window treatment is attached. The board is mounted either to the wall or inside the window casement at the top.

Pattern repeat: Distance between an element on one motif to an identical element on the next. Pattern is the total measurement of one complete design.

Piping: A decorative edging made of bias-cut fabric which encases cord.

Raw edge: The cut edge of fabric.

Return: The distance from the front of the rod to the brackets.

Rod pocket: Casing at the top of curtain or drape that fits over the rod.

Seam: Joining two pieces of fabric by sewing together.

Seam allowance: The amount of fabric used when sewing fabric pieces together.

Selvage: The tightly woven finished edge of fabric that runs down the length.

Spring tension rod: A rod that fits inside the window frame. The spring inside the rod makes it possible to adjust to correct size.

Take-up: The addition of the circumference of the rod to the cut length measurement.

Tie back: Fabric, rope or other materials to hold back the curtain.

Valance: A top treatment on a window that is short in length and can be hung alone or be mounted over draperies or curtains.